CW00727269

CHILDREN'S ENCYCLOPEDIA
HISTORY

CHILDREN'S ENCYCLOPEDIA
HISTORY

Miles Kelly

First published in 2014 by Miles Kelly Publishing Ltd
Harding's Barn, Bardfield End Green, Thaxted, Essex, CM6 3PX, UK

Copyright © Miles Kelly Publishing Ltd 2014

This edition printed 2015

2 4 6 8 10 9 7 5 3

Publishing Director Belinda Gallagher
Creative Director Jo Cowan
Cover Designer Simon Lee
Designers D&A, Rob Hale, Sally Lace, Louisa Leitao,
Joe Jones, Andrea Slane
Indexer Jane Parker
Image Manager Liberty Newton
Production Elizabeth Collins, Caroline Kelly
Reprographics Stephan Davis, Jennifer Cozens, Thom Allaway
Contributors Fiona Macdonald, John Malam,
Rupert Matthews, Jane Walker
Assets Lorraine King

ISBN 978-1-78209-184-4

Printed in China

British Library Cataloguing-in-Publication Data
A catalogue record for this book is available from the British Library

Made with paper from a sustainable forest

www.mileskelly.net
info@mileskelly.net

CONTENTS

ANCIENT GREECE 92–133

ANCIENT ROME 134–175

GLADIATORS

1 **Without the river Nile, the civilization of ancient Egypt might never have existed.** The Nile provided water for drinking and watering crops. Every year its floods left a strip of rich, dark soil on both sides of the river where farmers grew crops. The Egyptians called their country *Kemet*, which means 'black land', after this dark soil. The Nile was also a trade route.

▼ The Nile supported many activities such as trade and farming. It was also an important transportation route, with people and goods travelling by boat.

Powerful pharaohs

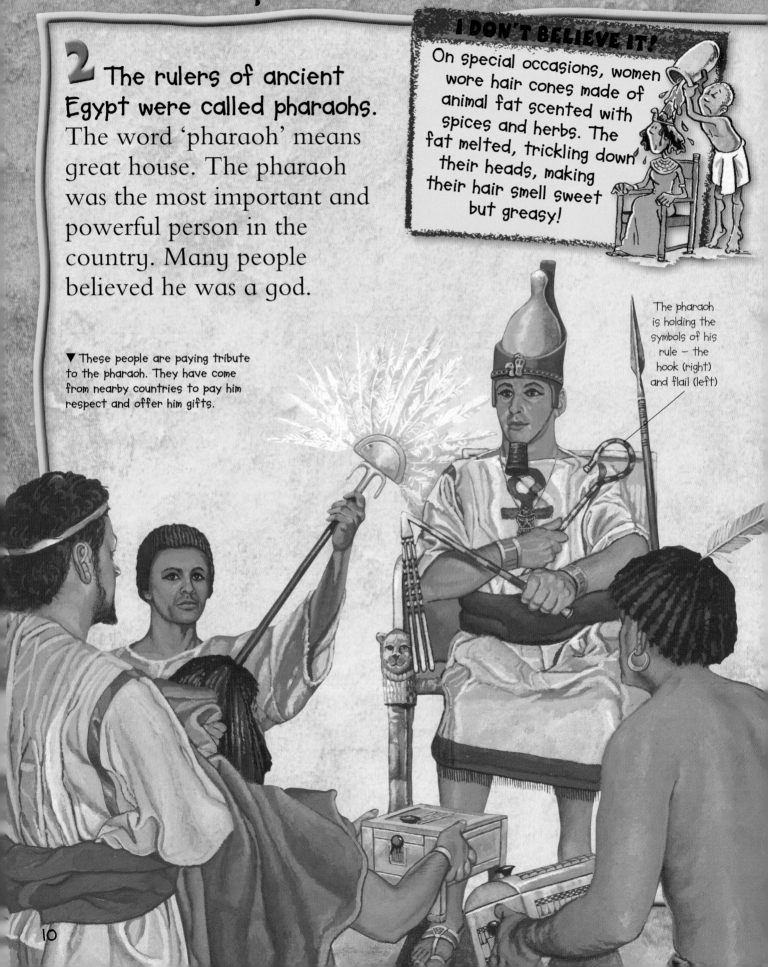

2 The rulers of ancient Egypt were called pharaohs. The word 'pharaoh' means great house. The pharaoh was the most important and powerful person in the country. Many people believed he was a god.

I DON'T BELIEVE IT!
On special occasions, women wore hair cones made of animal fat scented with spices and herbs. The fat melted, trickling down their heads, making their hair smell sweet but greasy!

▼ These people are paying tribute to the pharaoh. They have come from nearby countries to pay him respect and offer him gifts.

The pharaoh is holding the symbols of his rule – the hook (right) and flail (left)

◀ On her wedding day, the bride wore a long linen dress or tunic.

3 The pharaoh often married a close female relative, such as his sister or half-sister. In this way the blood of the royal family remained pure. The title of 'pharaoh' was usually passed on to the eldest son of the pharaoh's most important wife.

▲ At Abu Simbel Rameses II built four statues of himself, each over 20 metres tall.

4 Rameses II ruled for more than 60 years. He was the only pharaoh to carry the title 'the Great' after his name. Rameses was a great builder and brave soldier. He was also the father of a large number of children – 96 boys and 60 girls.

A civilization begins

5 More than 7000 years ago, people from Syria and the Sahara moved into Egypt. They learned how to farm crops, and settled in villages along the banks of the Nile and the Nile Delta. By about 5500 years ago, there were two kingdoms, Upper Egypt and Lower Egypt.

6 The history of ancient Egypt began more than 5000 years ago. The first period was called the Old Kingdom, when the Egyptians built the Great Pyramids. Next came the Middle Kingdom and finally the New Kingdom.

MEDITERRANEAN SEA
Nile Delta
Alexandria
Giza · Memphis
Saqqara
El-Amarna
LOWER EGYPT
Valley of the Kings · Karnak
Thebes · Luxor
· Aswan
· Abu Simbel
RED SEA
UPPER EGYPT
River Nile
NUBIAN DESERT

▲ Egypt was split into Lower Egypt (Nile Delta) and Upper Egypt (Nile Valley). Desert conditions meant that people settled along the banks of the Nile.

▼ Historians have divided Egyptian history into a number of periods depending on who was ruling Egypt at the time.

King Narmer, also called Menes, unites Egypt and records his deeds on the Narmer palette

Egypt's first pyramid, the Step Pyramid, was built in 2650 BC

People introduced gods for all different areas of life

The Hyksos people invaded in 1670 BC and introduced the chariot

Nilometers kept track of the height of the river, which was important for crops

3100–2750 BC
EARLY DYNASTIC PERIOD
(Dynasties I and II)

2750–2250 BC
OLD KINGDOM
(Dynasties III–VI)

2250–2025 BC
FIRST INTERMEDIATE PERIOD
(Dynasties VII–X)

2025–1627 BC
MIDDLE KINGDOM
(Dynasties XI–XIII)

1648–1539 BC
SECOND INTERMEDIATE PERIOD
(Dynasties XIV–XVII)

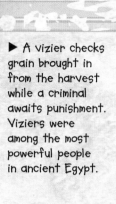

► A vizier checks grain brought in from the harvest while a criminal awaits punishment. Viziers were among the most powerful people in ancient Egypt.

7 Officials called viziers helped the pharaoh to govern Egypt. Each ruler appointed two viziers – one each for Upper and Lower Egypt. Each vizier was in charge of a number of royal overseers. Each overseer was responsible for a particular area of government, for example the army or granaries where the grain was stored.

8 Over 30 different dynasties ruled ancient Egypt. A dynasty is a line of rulers from the same family.

I DON'T BELIEVE IT!

Farmers tried to bribe tax collectors by offering them goats or ducks in exchange for a smaller tax charge.

The tomb of pharaoh Tutankhamun was discovered in 1922

The god Ra became Amun-Ra, the king of the gods

In 332 BC Alexander the Great conquered Egypt and founded the city of Alexandria

Queen Cleopatra was the last ruler of the Ptolemaic Period

The Roman Emperor Octavian conquered Egypt in 30 BC

1539–1070 BC
NEW KINGDOM
(Dynasties XVIII–XX)

1070–653 BC
THIRD INTERMEDIATE PERIOD
(Dynasties XXI–XXV)

664–332 BC
LATE PERIOD
(Dynasties XXVI–XXXI)

332–30 BC
PTOLEMAIC PERIOD

30 BC–AD 395
ROMAN PERIOD

Magnificent monuments

9 **The pyramids at Giza are more than 4500 years old.** They were built for three kings, Khufu, Khafre and Menkaure. The biggest, the Great Pyramid, took more than 20 years to build. Thousands of workers were needed to complete the job.

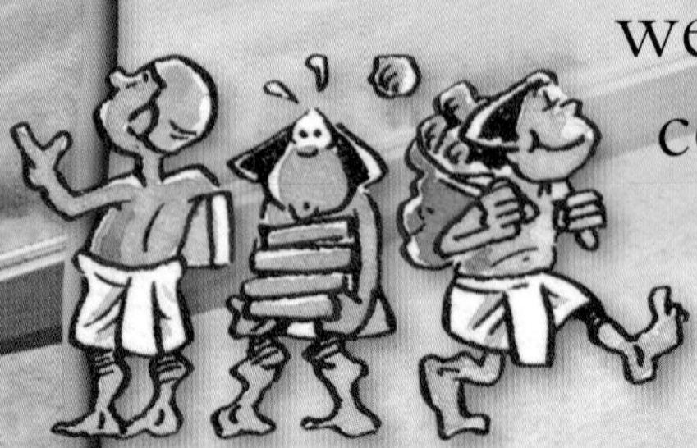

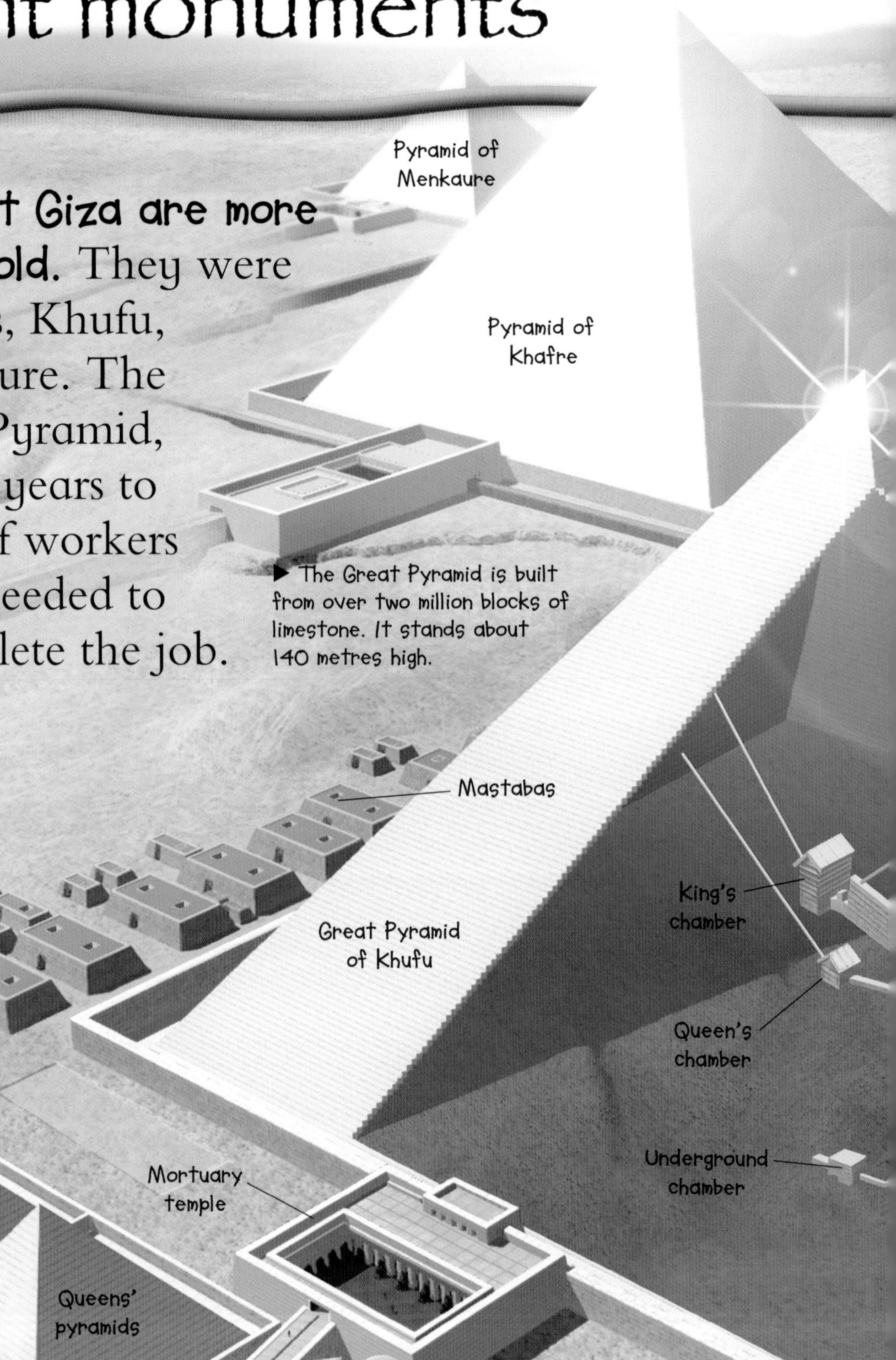

Pyramid of Menkaure

Pyramid of Khafre

▶ The Great Pyramid is built from over two million blocks of limestone. It stands about 140 metres high.

Mastabas

Great Pyramid of Khufu

King's chamber

Queen's chamber

Underground chamber

Mortuary temple

Queens' pyramids

10 **The Great Pyramid, the biggest of the three pyramids, was built as a burial place for King Khufu.** He ordered three smaller pyramids to be built beside it – for his three main wives. The boat that probably carried Khufu's body to his tomb was buried in a pit alongside the pyramid.

11 Inside the Great Pyramid were two burial rooms, for the pharaoh and his queen. The pharaoh's chamber was reached by a corridor called the Grand Gallery, with a roof more than 8 metres above the floor. Once the king's body was inside the chamber, the entrance was sealed with stone blocks. The last workers had to leave by specially built escape passages.

Western cemetery

Grand Gallery

Entrance

12 The Great Sphinx at Giza guards the way to Khafre's pyramid. It is a huge stone statue with the body of a lion and the head of a human.

▶ The features on the face of the Great Sphinx were carved to look like those of pharaoh Khafre.

13 Tomb robbers broke into the pyramids to steal the fabulous treasures inside. To make things difficult for the robbers, pyramid builders added heavy doors of granite and built false corridors.

14 The earliest pyramids had stepped sides. The steps were like a giant staircase, which the pharaoh could climb to reach the gods. The first step pyramid was built in the desert at Saqqara in about 2650 BC.

15

Supreme beings

15 **The ancient Egyptians worshipped many gods and goddesses.** The most important was Ra, the sun god. People believed that he was swallowed up each evening by the sky goddess Nut. During the night Ra travelled the underworld and was reborn each morning.

16 **A god was often shown as an animal, or as half-human, half-animal.** Bastet was goddess of cats, musicians and dancers. Cats were sacred in ancient Egypt. When a pet cat died, it was wrapped and laid in a cat-shaped coffin before burial in a cat cemetery. The moon god Thoth usually had the head of an ibis, but he was sometimes shown as a baboon. People believed that hieroglyphic writing came from Thoth.

Amun-Ra
Sun god

Nut
Sky goddess

▶ Crocodiles were kept at the temples of the god Sobek.

◀ The sun god Ra was popular in Lower Egypt. The people of Upper Egypt linked him to their own god Amun, so both gods became known as Amun-Ra.

Sobek
God of the Nile

Bastet
Goddess of cats and music

17
As god of the dead, Osiris was in charge of the underworld. Ancient Egyptians believed that dead people travelled to the kingdom of the underworld below the Earth. Osiris and his wife Isis were the parents of the god Horus, protector of the pharaoh.

18
Anubis was in charge of preparing bodies to be mummified. This work was known as embalming. Because jackals were often found near cemeteries, Anubis, who watched over the dead, was given the form of a jackal. Egyptian priests often wore Anubis masks.

19
Pharaoh Amenhotep IV worshipped one god – Aten the creator. He closed down temples to all other gods and even changed his name to Akhenaten, which means 'Spirit of Aten'.

Thoth
Moon god

Osiris
God of the dead

Horus
God of the sky

Isis
Goddess of rebirth

Anubis
God of the underworld

In tombs and temples

20 From about 2150 BC pharaohs were not buried in pyramids, but in tombs in the Valley of the Kings. This remote place was surrounded by steep cliffs on the west bank of the Nile opposite the city of Thebes. Some tombs were cut into the sides of the cliffs, others were built deep underground.

21 The riches in the tombs attracted robbers. The entrance to the Valley of the Kings was guarded, but robbers broke into every tomb except one within 1000 years. The only one they missed was the boy king Tutankhamun's, and even this had been partially robbed and re-sealed.

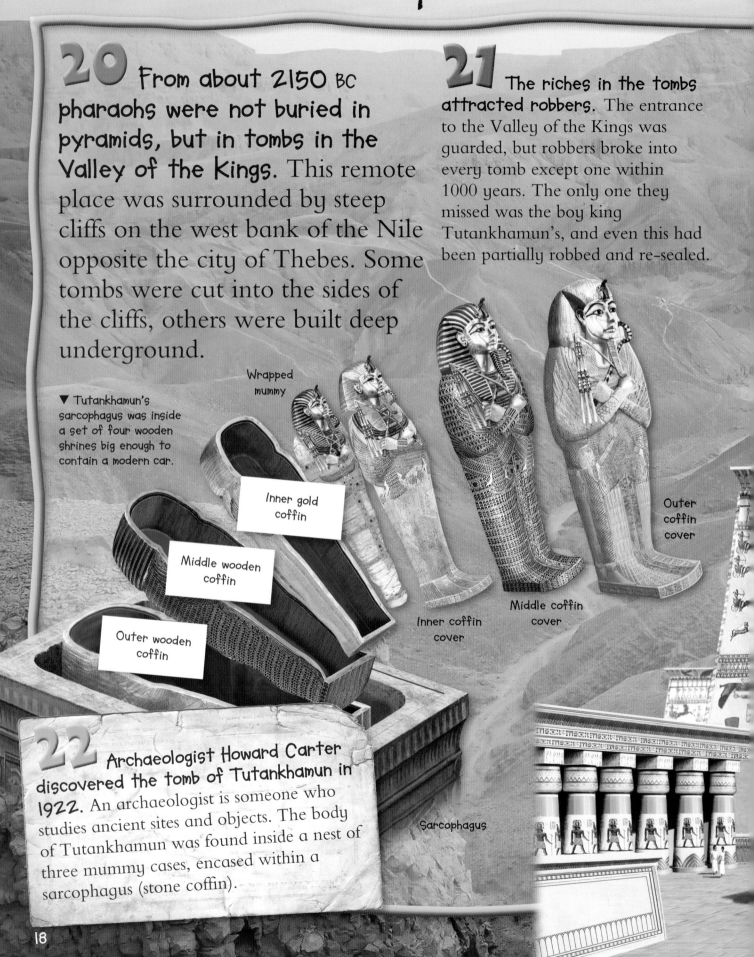

▼ Tutankhamun's sarcophagus was inside a set of four wooden shrines big enough to contain a modern car.

Wrapped mummy

Inner gold coffin

Middle wooden coffin

Outer wooden coffin

Inner coffin cover

Middle coffin cover

Outer coffin cover

Sarcophagus

22 Archaeologist Howard Carter discovered the tomb of Tutankhamun in 1922. An archaeologist is someone who studies ancient sites and objects. The body of Tutankhamun was found inside a nest of three mummy cases, encased within a sarcophagus (stone coffin).

23

The Egyptians built fabulous temples to worship their gods. Powerful priests ruled over the temples, and the riches and lands attached to them. Many of the finest temples were dedicated to Amun-Ra, king of the gods.

24

Building work at the Temples of Karnak lasted 1700 years from about 1900 BC. There were three great temples dedicated to the gods Amun-Re, Mut and Montu plus dozens of smaller temples and chapels. Today, millions of people flock to the area to see the remains of the once splendid temple structures.

▼ The courtyard in the Temple of Amun-Re at Karnak was entered through a massive gateway, or pylon, about 17 metres tall.

Big building blocks

25 Each block used to build the Great Pyramid weighed as much as two and a half adult elephants! Labourers used copper chisels and saws to cut and shape the stones before dragging them on wooden sledges to the base of the pyramid.

▶ Pyramids were built using large blocks of stone dragged into position by teams of workmen.

The finished pyramids had a bright, white casing of polished limestone to reflect the rays of the Sun, and the top may have been covered by gold leaf

The huge stones had to be levered into exactly the right position

Wooden sledge for dragging stone blocks

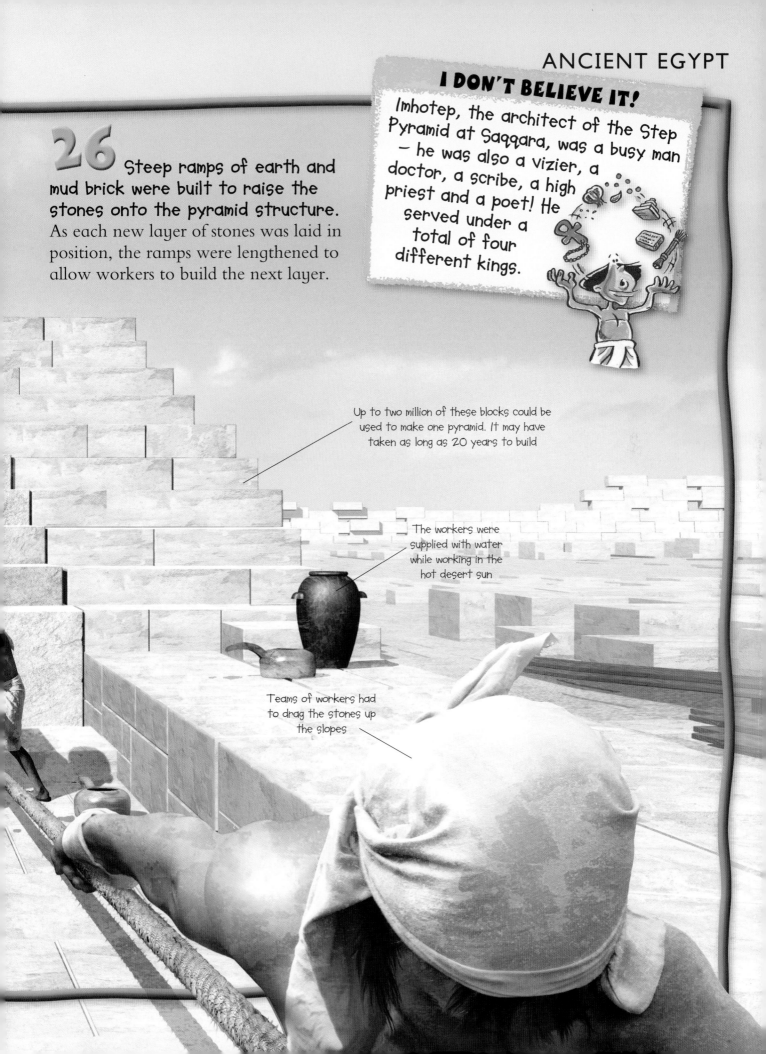

26 Steep ramps of earth and mud brick were built to raise the stones onto the pyramid structure. As each new layer of stones was laid in position, the ramps were lengthened to allow workers to build the next layer.

I DON'T BELIEVE IT!

Imhotep, the architect of the Step Pyramid at Saqqara, was a busy man — he was also a vizier, a doctor, a scribe, a high priest and a poet! He served under a total of four different kings.

Up to two million of these blocks could be used to make one pyramid. It may have taken as long as 20 years to build

The workers were supplied with water while working in the hot desert sun

Teams of workers had to drag the stones up the slopes

Making mummies

27 **Making a mummy was skilled work.** First the brain, stomach, lungs and other organs were removed, but the heart was left in place. Next, the body was covered with salts and left to dry for up to 40 days. The dried body was washed and filled with linen and other stuffing to keep its shape. Then it was oiled and wrapped in linen bandages.

29 **Animals were made into mummies too.** A nobleman might be buried with a mummy of his pet cat. Mummification was expensive, so people only preserved animals in this way to offer them to the gods. One mummified crocodile discovered by archaeologists was over 4.5 metres long.

Priest wearing Anubis mask reads prayers

Canopic jars used to store organs

Amulets (charms) placed inside bandages

28 **Body parts were removed from the dead person and stored in special containers.** The stomach, intestines, lungs and liver were cut out and stored in four separate containers called canopic jars.

30 A mask was fitted over the face of a mummy.

The ancient Egyptians believed that the mask would help the dead person's spirit to recognize the mummy later on. A pharaoh's mummy mask was made of gold and precious stones.

31 When ready for burial, a mummy was placed inside a special case.

Some cases were simple wooden boxes, but others were shaped like mummies and richly decorated. The mummy case of an important person, such as a pharaoh or a nobleman, was sealed inside a stone coffin called a sarcophagus.

▼ The process of making mummies took place in sacred workshops and was accompanied by rituals and prayers.

It took many years of training to become a mummy-maker

Hundreds of metres of bandages were used

23

War and enemies

32 Foot soldiers carried metal swords and spears, with shields made of wood or ox hide. Later, soldiers were protected by body armour made from strips of leather.

▼ A pharaoh, wearing the blue war crown, rides into battle on a chariot.

▶ During the New Kingdom, Egypt formed a professional army of trained soldiers. They had strong shields and long, deadly spears.

33 Soldiers fired arrows while riding in horse-drawn chariots. Each chariot carried two soldiers and was pulled by a pair of horses. During the time of the New Kingdom (around 3500 years ago), this new kind of war weapon helped the Egyptians to defeat several invading armies.

34 The Hyksos people conquered Egypt in about 1700 BC. They ruled the Egyptians for 200 years. They introduced the horse, the chariot and other new weapons that the Egyptians eventually used to conquer an empire.

35 A Macedonian general called Ptolemy won control of Egypt in 323 BC. He was the first of several rulers who made up the Ptolemaic dynasty. Under the Ptolemies, the city of Alexandria, on the Mediterranean Sea, became the new Egyptian capital and an important city for art and culture.

I DON'T BELIEVE IT!

Soldiers who fought bravely in battle were awarded golden fly medals – for 'buzzing' the enemy so successfully!

36 The Sea People attacked Egypt during the reign of Rameses III. These raiders came from the northeastern corner of the Mediterranean. Rameses sent a fleet of ships to defeat them.

◄ The great harbours at Alexandria were guarded by the huge Pharos, the first lighthouse in the world and one of the Seven Wonders of the Ancient World.

Bartering and buying

37 **Before 500 BC, Egyptian traders did not use money to buy and sell goods.** Instead they bartered (exchanged goods) with other traders. Merchants visited lands bordering the Mediterranean Sea as well as lands to the south. They offered goods such as gold, a paper called papyrus, and cattle.

38 **Egyptians traded with a large number of countries in the Middle East and Africa.** Traders brought back silver from Syria, cedar wood, oils and horses from Lebanon, copper from Cyprus, a gem called lapis lazuli from Afghanistan, and ebony wood and ivory from central Africa.

I DON'T BELIEVE IT!

Fly swatters made from giraffe tails were a popular fashion item in ancient Egypt.

39 Merchants brought back exotic goods from the land of Nubia, to the south of Egypt. These included leopard skins, elephant tusks, ostrich feathers – and slaves. One of the main trading posts where goods were exchanged was the town of Kerma, on the river Nile beyond Egypt.

▶ A painting shows men from Nubia bringing goods to Egypt.

▲ A busy Egyptian trading market with people bartering for goods.

40 When goods were sold they were weighed using a balance and special copper weights called deben. An item could be exchanged for its equivalent weight in copper. A bed, for example, had a value of 25 deben. Pieces of gold and silver were also weighed and used as payment.

The farmer's year

41 **The farming year was divided into three seasons: the flood, the growing period and the harvest.** Most people worked on the land, but farmers could not work between July and November because the land was flooded. Instead, they helped to build the pyramids and royal palaces.

▲ Water is lifted onto a field using a shaduf, just as is done in Egypt today.

42 **The river Nile used to flood its banks in July each year.** The flood waters left a strip of rich, black soil, about 10 kilometres wide, along each bank. Apart from these fertile strips and a few scattered oases (pools of water in the desert) the rest of the land was mainly just sand.

44 **Water was lifted from the Nile using a shaduf.** It was a long pole with a wooden bucket hanging from a rope at one end, and a weight at the other. The pole was supported by a wooden frame. One person working alone could operate a shaduf.

◀ Tax collectors would often decide how rich a person was by counting how many cattle he owned.

43 **Egyptian farmers had to water their crops because of the hot, dry climate with no rain.** They dug special channels around their fields along which the waters of the Nile could flow. In this way farmers could water their crops all year round. This was called irrigation.

▲ Almost no rain fell on the dry, dusty farmland of ancient Egypt. No crops could grow properly without the water from the Nile.

45 Wooden ploughs pulled by oxen prepared the soil for planting. Seeds were mainly planted by hand. At harvest time, wooden sickles edged with stone teeth were used to cut the crops.

▲ A man ploughs a field of wheat or barley, assisted by his wife.

46 Harvesting grain was only the start of the process. In the threshing room people would beat the grain to separate it from the chaff, the shell, of the grain. It was then winnowed. Men would throw the grain and chaff into the air and fan away the chaff. The heavier grain dropped straight to the floor. The grain was then gathered up and taken to the granary to be stored.

47 Wheat and barley (for bread and beer) were the two main crops grown by the ancient Egyptians. They also grew grapes (for wine) and flax (to make linen). A huge variety of fruits and vegetables grew in the fertile soil, including dates, figs, cucumbers, melons, onions, peas, leeks and lettuces.

▼ Winnowers separate the grain from the chaff.

I DON'T BELIEVE IT!

Instead of using scarecrows, Egyptian farmers hired young boys to scare away the birds — they had to have a loud voice and a good aim with a slingshot!

48 Egyptian farmers kept cattle as well as goats, sheep, ducks and geese. Some farmers kept bees to produce honey, which was used for sweetening cakes and other foods.

Getting around

49 The main method of transporting goods in ancient Egypt was by boat along the Nile. The Nile is the world's longest river. It flows across the entire length of the desert lands of Egypt.

50 The earliest kinds of boat were made from papyrus reeds. They were propelled by a long pole and, later on, by oars. Gradually, wooden boats replaced the reed ones, and sails were added.

▲ Early boats were made from bundles of reeds tied together.

51 A magnificent carved boat was built to carry the body of King Khufu at his funeral. More than 43 metres long, it was built from planks of cedar wood. The boat was buried in a special pit next to the Great Pyramid.

▲ The Nile results from the joining of three great rivers — the White Nile, the Blue Nile and the Atbara.

52 Transporting cattle across the Nile could be difficult. Wide-bodied cargo boats were used to ferry cattle across the Nile. The animals stood on the deck during the crossing.

◄ In 1954, King Khufu's funerary boat was found buried at the foot of the Great Pyramid.

53

Wooden barges carried blocks of limestone across the river Nile for the pyramids and temples. The stone came from quarries on the opposite bank to the site of the pyramids. The granite used to build the insides of the pyramids came from much farther away – from quarries at Aswan 800 kilometres upstream.

▼ A merchant river boat powered by sails or oars.

▲ Blocks of stone are loaded on a boat to be taken along the Nile to a building site.

Who's who?

54 People were divided into classes. Farmers and tradesmen worked in businesses owned by the state or temples, and could not move class. Scribes and merchants could move, but were barely richer than farmers and tradesmen. Nobles and priests organized Egypt under the pharaoh's rule.

◀ The arrangement of Egyptian society can be shown as a pyramid shape. The pharaoh sits at the top, with unskilled labourers at the bottom.

Viziers and priests

Scribes and noblemen

Craftworkers and dancers

Peasant workers

55 The man was the head of the household. On his father's death, the eldest son inherited the family's land and riches. Women had rights and privileges too. They could own property and carry out business deals, and women from wealthy families could become doctors or priestesses.

▶ Family life played an important role in ancient Egypt. Couples could adopt children if they were unable to have their own.

I DON'T BELIEVE IT!

Wealthy Egyptians wanted servants in the afterlife too. They were buried with models of servants, called shabtis, that were meant to come to life and look after their dead owner!

56 Most ancient Egyptians lived along the banks of the river Nile or in the river valley. As Egypt became more powerful they spread out, up along the river Nile and around the Mediterranean Sea. Others lived by oases, pools of water in the desert.

57 Rich families had several servants, who worked as maids, cooks and gardeners. In large houses the servants had their own quarters separate from those of the family.

58 Dogs and cats were the main pets. Egyptians also kept pet monkeys and sometimes flocks of tame doves. Some people trained their pet baboons to climb fig trees and pick the ripe fruits.

59 Young children played with wooden and clay toys. Popular toys were carved animals – often with moving parts – spinning tops, toy horses, dolls and clay balls. Children also played games that are still played today, such as leapfrog and tug-o'-war.

Home sweet home

60 Houses were made from mud bricks dried in the sun. Straw and pebbles were added to the mud to make it strong. Tree trunks supported the flat roofs. Inside walls were plastered and often painted. The rich lived in big houses with several storeys. The poor often lived in a single room.

61 Rich families lived in spacious villas in the countryside. A typical villa had a pond filled with fish, a walled garden and an orchard of fruit trees.

62 Homes were furnished with wooden chairs, tables, chests and carved beds. A three- or four-legged footstool was a common item of furniture. Reed mats covered the floors.

Pots and plates were made of clay and fired in a hot kiln.

Bricks were made of mud and clay strengthened with straw and pebbles. They were packed in wooden frames and left to harden in the sun.

63 Food was cooked in a clay oven or over an open fire. Most kitchens had a cylinder-shaped oven made from bricks of baked clay. Wood or charcoal was burnt as fuel, and food was placed in two-handled pottery saucepans to cook.

64 Pottery lamps provided lighting. The container was filled with oil and a wick made of cotton or flax was burned. Houses had very small windows, and sometimes none at all, so there was often little natural light. Small windows kept out the strong sunlight, helping to keep houses cool.

Bread was the staple food. It was baked in a hot oven. The poor ate coarse brown bread and the rich ate white.

Beer was stored in pottery jars. Spices and dates were added to improve the taste.

Clothes were made with linen woven on a loom, from the fibres of the flax plant.

65 In most Egyptian homes there was a small shrine. Here, members of the family worshipped their household god.

66 In Egypt it was good to eat with your fingers! In rich households, servants would even bring jugs of water between courses so that people could rinse their hands.

Dressing up

67 **Egyptians wore lucky charms called amulets.** The charms were meant to protect the wearer from evil spirits and to bring good luck. One of the most popular ones was the eye of the god Horus. Children wore amulets shaped like fish to protect them from drowning in the river Nile.

▲ Scarab amulets were worn for good fortune. They were carved from gems and semi-precious stones.

68 **Both men and women wore eye make-up.** A black eye make-up, called kohl, was made from ground-up raw metals mixed with oil. The Egyptians believed it had healing powers and could restore bad eyesight and fight infections. People also used rouge for the cheeks and lips, face powder, paint for fingernails and hair dyes.

◄ A wealthy woman applying eye make-up before putting on her wig.

69 **Most clothes were made from light-coloured linen.** Women wore long dresses, often with pleated cloaks. Noblewomen's dresses were made of the best cloth with beads sewn onto it. Noblemen wore either robes or kilt-like skirts, a piece of linen wrapped around the waist and tied in a decorative knot.

▶ Wealthy Egyptians wore long robes of pleated linen.

70 **Sandals were made from papyrus and other reeds.** Kings and queens, rich people and courtiers wore padded leather ones. Footwear was a luxury item, and most ordinary people walked around barefoot. Colourful pictures of sandals were even painted onto the feet of mummies!

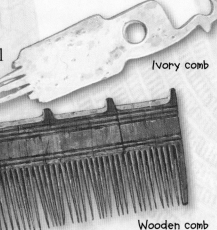

Ivory hair pins

Wooden comb

Ivory comb

MAKE A MAGIC EYE CHARM

You will need:
self-hardening modelling clay
length of leather strip or thick cord
pencil   poster paints
paintbrush   varnish

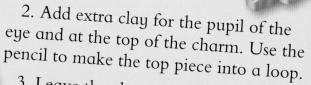

1. Knead the clay until soft and then shape into the charm.

2. Add extra clay for the pupil of the eye and at the top of the charm. Use the pencil to make the top piece into a loop.

3. Leave the clay to harden. Paint in bright colours and leave to dry.

4. Varnish, then thread the leather strip or cord through the loop and wear your charm for extra luck.

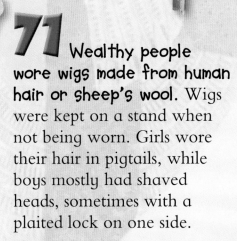

▶ Wigs were often long and elaborate and needed a lot of care.

▼ Egyptians cared for their wigs with combs made of wood and ivory. They used ivory pins to keep their hair in place.

71 **Wealthy people wore wigs made from human hair or sheep's wool.** Wigs were kept on a stand when not being worn. Girls wore their hair in pigtails, while boys mostly had shaved heads, sometimes with a plaited lock on one side.

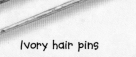

37

Baking and brewing

72 **Bread was the most important food.** Harvested grain was stored in granaries until needed. Beer was the most popular drink. It was very thick and had to be strained before drinking. Models of brewers were left in tombs to ensure the dead person had plenty of beer in the next world!

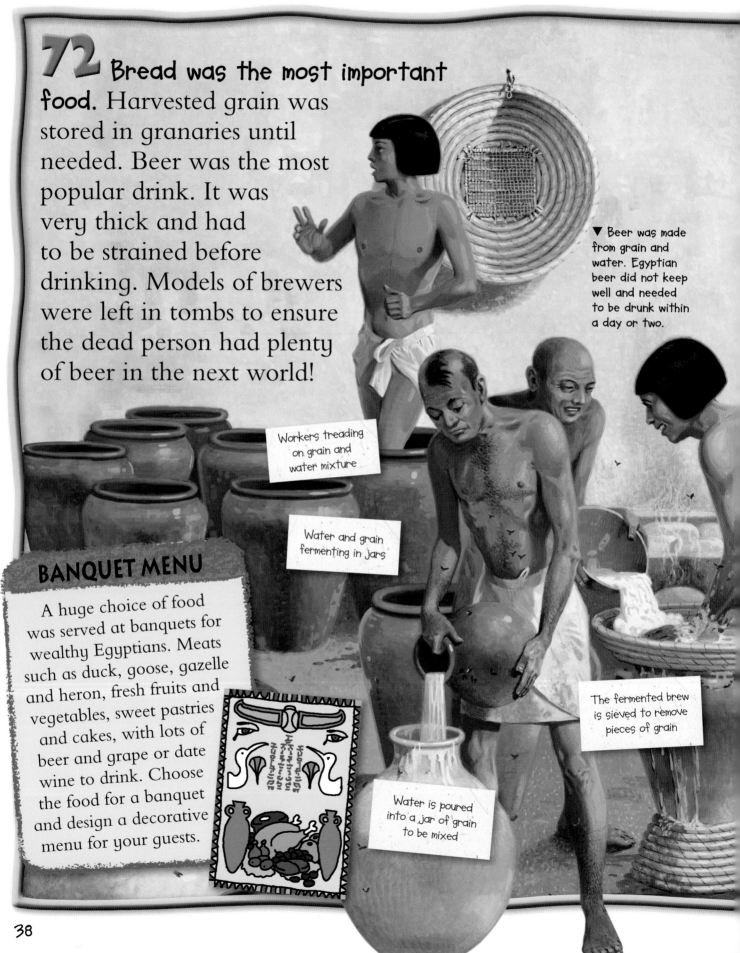

▼ Beer was made from grain and water. Egyptian beer did not keep well and needed to be drunk within a day or two.

Workers treading on grain and water mixture

Water and grain fermenting in jars

The fermented brew is sieved to remove pieces of grain

Water is poured into a jar of grain to be mixed

BANQUET MENU

A huge choice of food was served at banquets for wealthy Egyptians. Meats such as duck, goose, gazelle and heron, fresh fruits and vegetables, sweet pastries and cakes, with lots of beer and grape or date wine to drink. Choose the food for a banquet and design a decorative menu for your guests.

73 **A rough kind of bread was baked from wheat or barley.** It often contained gritty pieces that wore down people's teeth. Historians have discovered this by studying the teeth of mummies.

Bread dough is kneaded to make the mix supple and nutritious

An overseer ensured the quality of the finished product

Grain could be made into flour by pounding or by grinding

▲ Bread was made from grain that had been ground into flour and mixed with water. It could be stored for a few days before being eaten.

Hard day's work

74 Scribes were very important people. These highly skilled men kept records of everything that happened from day to day. They recorded the materials used for building work, the number of cattle, and the crops that had been gathered for the royal family, the government and the temples.

75 Libraries in ancient Egypt held thousands of papyrus scrolls. They covered subjects such as law, astronomy, medicine and geography Most Egyptians could not read or write, so libraries were used by educated people such as scribes and doctors.

76 Imagine if there were 700 letters in the alphabet! That was how many hieroglyphs Egyptian school children had to learn. Hieroglyphs were symbols that the Egyptians used for writing. Some symbols stood for words and some for sounds. Only boys went to schools for scribes, where they first learned how to read and write hieroglyphs.

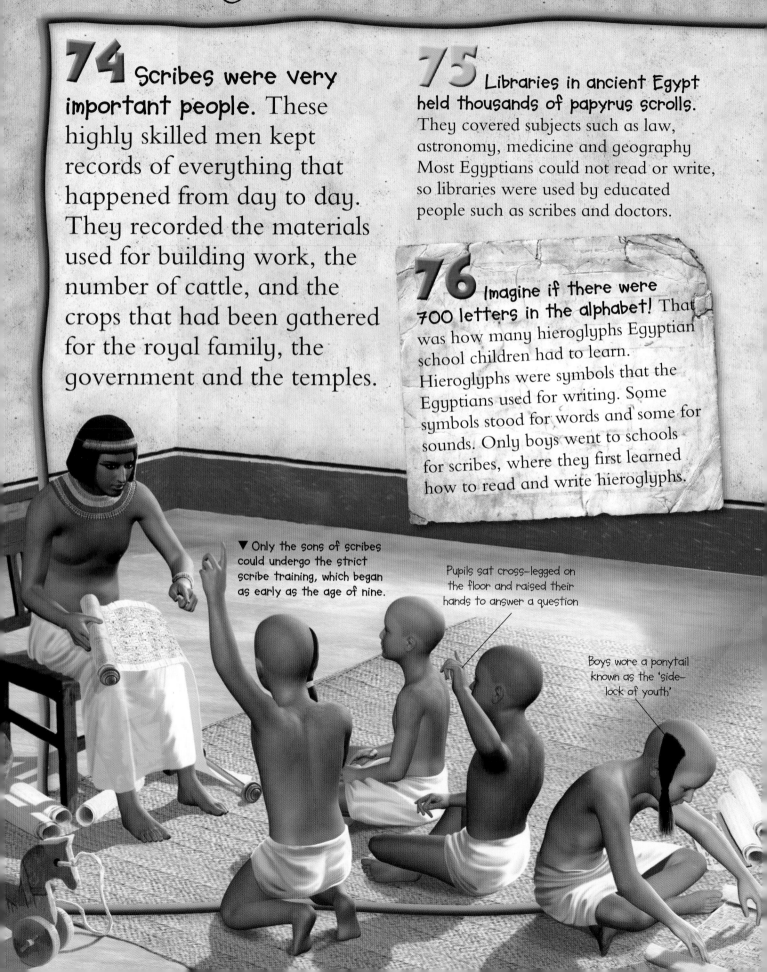

▼ Only the sons of scribes could undergo the strict scribe training, which began as early as the age of nine.

Pupils sat cross-legged on the floor and raised their hands to answer a question

Boys wore a ponytail known as the 'side-lock of youth'

77
Most people worked as craftworkers or farm labourers. Craftworkers included carpenters, potters, weavers, jewellers, shoemakers, glassblowers and perfume makers. Many sold their goods from small shops in the towns. They were kept busy making items for the pharaoh and wealthy people.

▶ Craftworkers produced statues and furniture for the pharaoh. Workers such as these often had their own areas within a town. The village of Deir el-Medina was built specially for those who worked on tombs in the Valley of the Kings.

78
A typical lunch for a worker consisted of bread and onions. They may also have had a cucumber, washed down with a drink of beer.

80
Slaves were often prisoners who were captured from enemies. They also came from the countries of Kush and Nubia. Life as a slave was not all bad. A slave could own land and buy goods – and even buy his freedom.

79
The base of the Great Pyramid takes up almost as much space as five football pitches!
Huge quantities of stone were needed to build these monuments. The Egyptians quarried limestone, sandstone and granite for their buildings. In the surrounding desert they mined gold for decorations.

QUIZ
1. Were girls sent to scribe school?
2. Where did Egyptians get their slaves?
3. Who used libraries?
4. Where was gold found?

Answers:
1. No, only boys 2. From Kush and Nubia 3. Scribes and doctors 4. In the deserts of Egypt

Clever Egyptians

81 The insides of many Egyptian tombs were decorated with brightly coloured wall paintings. The scenes showed what the Egyptians hoped life in the next world would be like.

▲ The Egyptians believed that these wall paintings would come to life in the next world.

82 Sculptors carved enormous statues of their pharaohs and gods. Stone statues up to 20 metres tall were placed outside tombs or temples to guard the entrance. Inside a tomb was a small wooden statue of the dead person where the ka, or life force, of the person could rest. Inside temples the holiest statue of a god would be made of silver, ivory or gold.

▲ Huge stone statues guard the entrance to the temple of Abu Simbel. When the temple was rediscovered in 1817, it was almost covered by sand.

83 There were three different calendars.

A 365-day farming calendar was made up of three seasons of four months. An astronomical calendar was based on observations of the star Sirius, which reappeared at the start of the flood season. Priests kept a calendar based on the movements of the Moon, which told them when to perform ceremonies for the moon god.

84 Astronomers recorded what they saw in the night skies.

The Egyptian calendar was based on the movement of Sirius, the brightest star in the sky. The Egyptians used their knowledge of astronomy to build temples that lined up with certain stars.

85 Nilometers were used to study the annual river floods.

As the water rose it entered a chamber marked with lines to measure the height of the flood and where priests could see how much mud the flood was bringing.

▶ A doctor consults a papyrus roll while treating a patient.

86 Egyptian doctors knew how to set broken bones and treat illnesses such as fevers.

They used medicines made from plants such as garlic and juniper to treat sick people. The Egyptians had a good knowledge of the basic workings of the human body.

43

From pictures to words

87 The Egyptians had no paper – they wrote on papyrus. It was made from papyrus reeds that grew on the banks of the Nile. At first papyrus was sold as long strips, or scrolls, tied with string. Later, papyrus sheets were put into books. Papyrus lasts a long time – sheets have survived 3000 years to the present day.

88 Ink was made by mixing water with soot, charcoal or coloured minerals. Scribes wrote in ink on papyrus scrolls, using reed brushes with specially shaped ends.

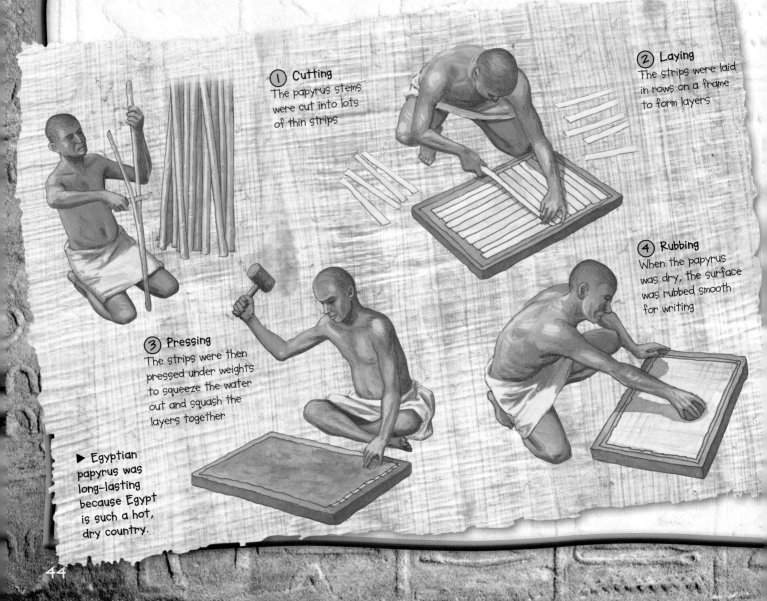

① **Cutting**
The papyrus stems were cut into lots of thin strips

② **Laying**
The strips were laid in rows on a frame to form layers

④ **Rubbing**
When the papyrus was dry, the surface was rubbed smooth for writing

③ **Pressing**
The strips were then pressed under weights to squeeze the water out and squash the layers together

▶ Egyptian papyrus was long–lasting because Egypt is such a hot, dry country.

89 **The Rosetta Stone was found in 1799 by a French soldier in Egypt.** It is a large stone onto which three kinds of writing have been carved: hieroglyphics, demotics (a simpler form of hieroglyphics), and Greek. All three sets of writing give an account of the coronation of King Ptolemy V.

▲ The Rosetta Stone in the British Museum. The stone itself is made of granite, and is a broken part of a bigger slab.

90 **In the 5th century BC a Greek historian called Herodotus wrote about life in ancient Egypt.** As he travelled across the country he observed and wrote about people's daily lives, and their religion and customs such as embalming and mummification.

▼ The name of Rameses II written inside a cartouche to show he was a pharaoh.

91 **The hieroglyphs of a ruler's name were written inside an oval-shaped frame called a cartouche.** The pharaoh's cartouche was carved on pillars and temple walls, painted on tomb walls and mummy cases, and written on official documents.

92 **The Egyptians used a system of picture writing called hieroglyphics.** Each hieroglyph represented an object or a sound. For example, the picture of a lion represented the sound 'l' and a basket represented the word 'lord'. Scribes wrote hieroglyphs on papyrus scrolls or carved them into stone.

PICTURE-WRITING

Below is a hieroglyphic alphabet. The name 'Jane' has been written in hieroglyphs. Can you write your name?

Fun and games

93 Hippo hunting was a dangerous but popular sport. Hunters in boats, armed only with spears and ropes, killed hippos in the waters of the Nile. In the desert, hunters chased lions, antelope and wild bulls. Marsh birds were killed with throwing sticks that were like boomerangs.

MAKE A SNAKE GAME

You will need:

sheet of thick cardboard   large dinner plate
paintbrush   scissors   coloured pens
yellow paint   counters   pencil   two dice

Place the plate on the card and draw round the outside. Ask an adult to help cut out the circle. Paint one side with paint. Leave to dry.

Draw a snake's head in the centre of the circle. Draw small circles spreading out from the centre until you reach the edge of the cardboard. Colour the circles in.

Give each player a counter. Throw the dice and take turns to move along the circles. The winner is the first one to reach the snake's head.

▼ Hunting was reserved mostly for royalty and courtiers. Amenhotep III was said to have killed more than 100 lions in ten years.

94 The Egyptians played a board game called senet.

The game represented the struggle between good and evil on the journey into the next world. Players moved sets of counters across the board according to how their throwing sticks (like modern dice) landed.

▶ A senet game found in an Egyptian tomb.

Heroes and heroines

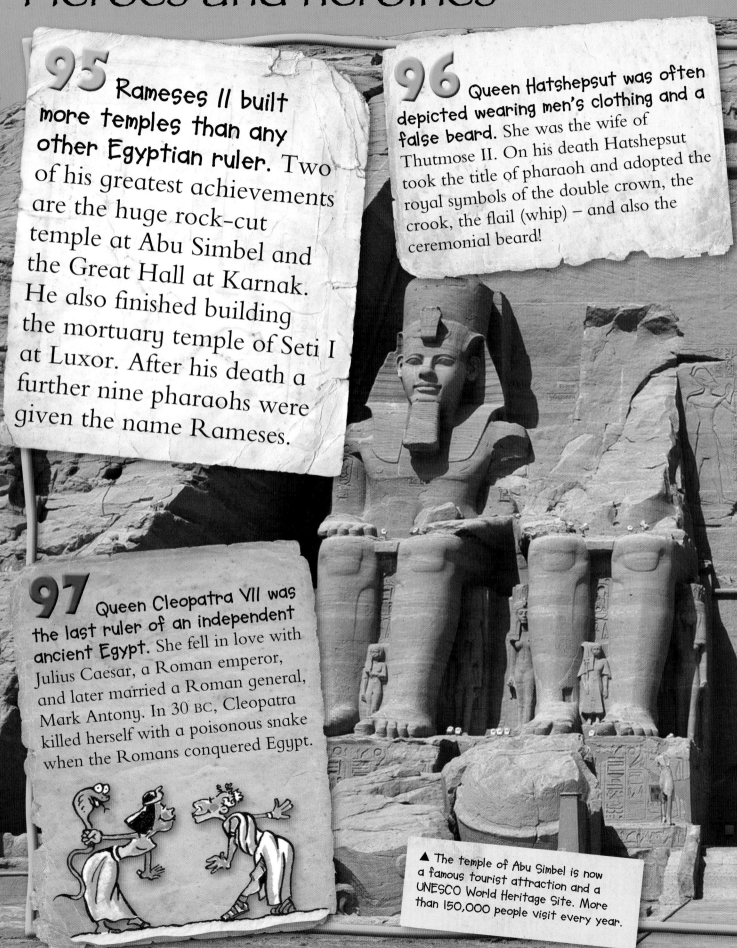

95 **Rameses II built more temples than any other Egyptian ruler.** Two of his greatest achievements are the huge rock-cut temple at Abu Simbel and the Great Hall at Karnak. He also finished building the mortuary temple of Seti I at Luxor. After his death a further nine pharaohs were given the name Rameses.

96 **Queen Hatshepsut was often depicted wearing men's clothing and a false beard.** She was the wife of Thutmose II. On his death Hatshepsut took the title of pharaoh and adopted the royal symbols of the double crown, the crook, the flail (whip) – and also the ceremonial beard!

97 **Queen Cleopatra VII was the last ruler of an independent ancient Egypt.** She fell in love with Julius Caesar, a Roman emperor, and later married a Roman general, Mark Antony. In 30 BC, Cleopatra killed herself with a poisonous snake when the Romans conquered Egypt.

▲ The temple of Abu Simbel is now a famous tourist attraction and a UNESCO World Heritage Site. More than 150,000 people visit every year.

98 Tutankhamun is probably the most famous pharaoh of all. His tomb, with its fabulous treasure of over 5000 objects, was discovered complete in 1922. Tutankhamun was only nine years old when he became ruler, and he died at the young age of about 17. He was buried in the Valley of the Kings.

▶ The head of of Tutankhamun's mummy was covered by a mask made of solid gold, and decorated with jewels.

99 King Menes was the first ruler of a united Egypt. He joined together the kingdoms of Upper and Lower Egypt, under one government, in around 3100 BC. Menes was also called Narmer. Archaeologists have found a slate tablet, called the Narmer Palette, that shows him beating his enemies in battle.

100 Thutmose III was a clever general who added new lands to ancient Egypt. Under his leadership, Egypt's armies seized territory in Syria to the north and Palestine to the east. During his reign Thutmose ordered a giant obelisk made of granite to be placed at Heliopolis – it now stands on the bank of the river Thames in London.

MUMMIES

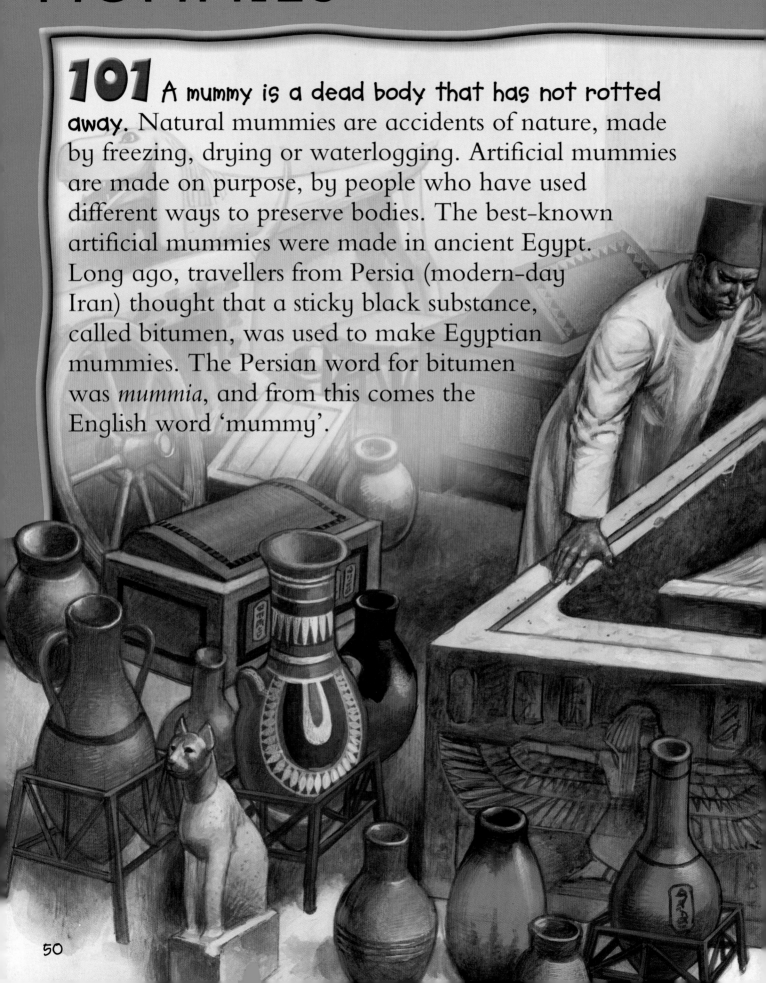

101 **A mummy is a dead body that has not rotted away.** Natural mummies are accidents of nature, made by freezing, drying or waterlogging. Artificial mummies are made on purpose, by people who have used different ways to preserve bodies. The best-known artificial mummies were made in ancient Egypt. Long ago, travellers from Persia (modern-day Iran) thought that a sticky black substance, called bitumen, was used to make Egyptian mummies. The Persian word for bitumen was *mummia*, and from this comes the English word 'mummy'.

▲ The 3300-year-old mummy of Egyptian pharaoh Tutankhamun was discovered in 1922 by Howard Carter. This is a good example of an artificial mummy.

The first mummies

102 The first artificial mummies were made 7000 years ago by the Chinchorro people of South America. These people are named after a place in Chile. Here, scientists discovered traces of the way the Chinchorro lived. They were a fishing people who lived along the coast of the Pacific Ocean.

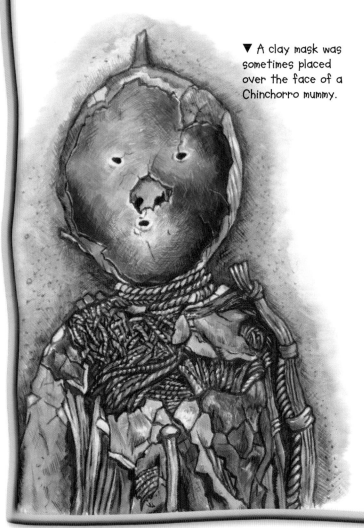

▼ A clay mask was sometimes placed over the face of a Chinchorro mummy.

QUIZ

1. Where did the Chinchorro people live?
2. What was put on a mummy to make a body shape?
3. For how many years did the Chinchorro make mummies?
4. When were the first mummies discovered?

Answers:
1. Chile in South America
2. White mud 3. 3000 years 4. 1917

103 It is thought that the Chinchorro made mummies because they believed in life after death. They tried to make a mummy look as lifelike as possible, which shows they did not want the person's body to rot away. Perhaps they thought the dead could live again if their bodies were preserved.

104 To make a mummy, the Chinchorro first removed all of a dead person's insides. The skin and flesh were then taken off the bones, which were left to dry. Then sticks were tied to the arm, leg and spine bones to hold them together. White mud was spread over the skeleton to build a body shape. The face skin was put back in place, and patches of skin were added to the body. When the mud was dry, it was painted black or red.

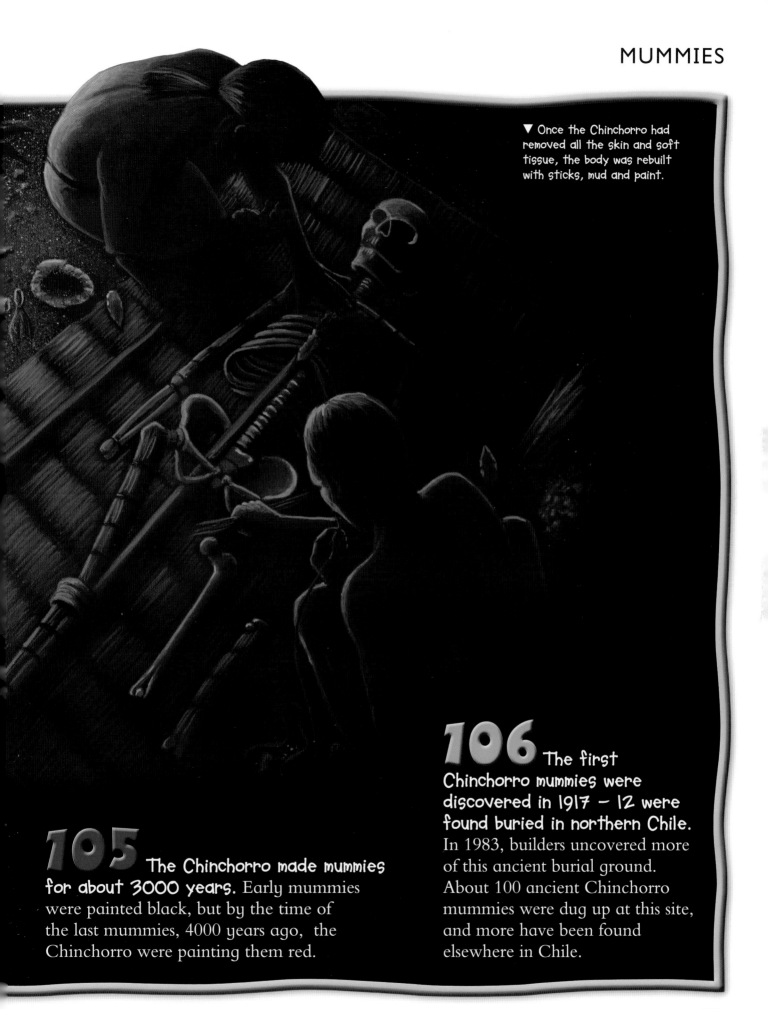

▼ Once the Chinchorro had removed all the skin and soft tissue, the body was rebuilt with sticks, mud and paint.

106 The first Chinchorro mummies were discovered in 1917 – 12 were found buried in northern Chile. In 1983, builders uncovered more of this ancient burial ground. About 100 ancient Chinchorro mummies were dug up at this site, and more have been found elsewhere in Chile.

105 The Chinchorro made mummies for about 3000 years. Early mummies were painted black, but by the time of the last mummies, 4000 years ago, the Chinchorro were painting them red.

Iceman of Europe

107 Europe's oldest human mummy is known as the Iceman. He died about 5300 years ago, at the end of the Stone Age. His mummy was discovered by hikers in northern Italy in 1991. They found it lying face down in an icy glacier.

108 The Iceman mummy was found high up in the mountains, where it is very cold. At first, people thought that he was a shepherd, or a hunter on the search for food – or even a traveller on a journey. Then in 2001, an arrowhead was found in the Iceman's left shoulder. He might have fled into the mountains to escape danger.

109 When the Iceman was alive, arrows had sharp points made from flint (a type of stone). It was a flint arrowhead that injured the Iceman, piercing his clothes and entering his left shoulder. This arrow caused a deep wound. The Iceman pulled the long arrow shaft out, but the arrowhead remained inside his body. This injury would have made the Iceman weak, eventually causing him to die.

◄ The Iceman is the oldest complete human mummy ever to be found. He is so well preserved, even his eyes are still visible.

110 The mummy's clothes were also preserved by the ice. For the first time, scientists saw how a Stone Age person actually dressed. The Iceman wore leggings and shoes made from leather, a goatskin coat, a bearskin hat and a cape made from woven grass. These would have kept the Iceman warm in the cold climate.

111 **Equipment used by the Iceman was also found with him.** He carried a copper axe, a flint dagger, and a bow and quiver with 14 arrows. He also had a leather pouch filled with dried grass, which he would have used for starting fires. If the Iceman had been a hunter, he would have killed animals, such as the mountain ibex (a type of goat) with his arrows.

112 **Today, the Iceman mummy and his clothes and equipment are kept at a museum in northern Italy.** Visitors are able to peep through a tiny window to see the Iceman, who is kept frozen inside a special room. The mummy must never be allowed to thaw, as this would cause it to rot.

▶ This reconstruction of the Iceman shows how he would have looked on the day he died.

Quiver to hold arrows

Leather pouch

Flint dagger

Copper axe

Shoes stuffed with grass for warmth

I DON'T BELIEVE IT!

At first, the Iceman was thought to be a modern person who had died in a recent accident on the mountain.

Bog bodies

113 Lots of mummies have been found in the peat bogs of northern Europe. Peat is a soily substance that is formed from plants that have fallen into pools of water. The plants sink to the bottom and are slowly turned into peat. If a dead body is placed in a bog, it may be preserved as a mummy. This is because there is little oxygen or bacteria to rot the body.

▶ The face of Tollund Man is so well preserved, he looks as if he is sleeping.

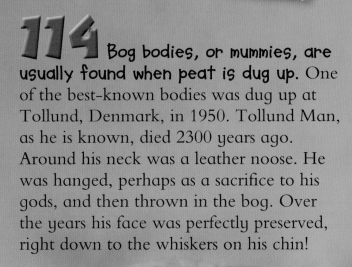

114 Bog bodies, or mummies, are usually found when peat is dug up. One of the best-known bodies was dug up at Tollund, Denmark, in 1950. Tollund Man, as he is known, died 2300 years ago. Around his neck was a leather noose. He was hanged, perhaps as a sacrifice to his gods, and then thrown in the bog. Over the years his face was perfectly preserved, right down to the whiskers on his chin!

115 Grauballe Man was also found in a peat bog in Denmark. He was discovered by peat workers near the village of Grauballe in 1852. About 2300 years ago, the man's throat was cut and he bled to death. His body was thrown into a bog, where it was preserved until its discovery.

▲ The head of Grauballe Man. Like all bog bodies, his skin has turned brown due to the acids in the bog.

116 Bog bodies have also been discovered in Germany. At Windeby, the body of a teenage girl was found. The girl, who died 1900 years ago, was wearing a blindfold. It seems she was taken to the bog, her eyes were covered, and then she was drowned. A heavy rock and branches were put on top of her body, so it sank to the bottom of the bog.

▶ The mummy of Windeby Girl revealed that some of her hair had been cut off, or shaved, at the time of her death.

117 From the Netherlands comes the bog body of another teenage girl. Known as Yde (*ay-de*) Girl, she was stabbed, strangled and then dumped in a bog around 1900 years ago. A medical artist made a copy of her skull, then covered it with wax to rebuild her face. The model shows scientists how Yde Girl may have looked when she was alive.

Lindow Man

118 A bog body of a man was found in north-west England in 1984. It was discovered by peat cutters at Lindow Moss, Cheshire. The mummy was named 'Lindow Man', but a local newspaper nicknamed it 'Pete Marsh' because a peat bog is a wet, marshy place! Lindow Man is now on display at the British Museum, London.

119 Lindow Man was about 20 years old when he died. His short life came to an end around 1900 years ago. After his death, his body was put in a bog, where it sank without trace until its discovery by the peat cutters.

▼ The body of Lindow Man was squashed flat by the weight of the peat on top of it.

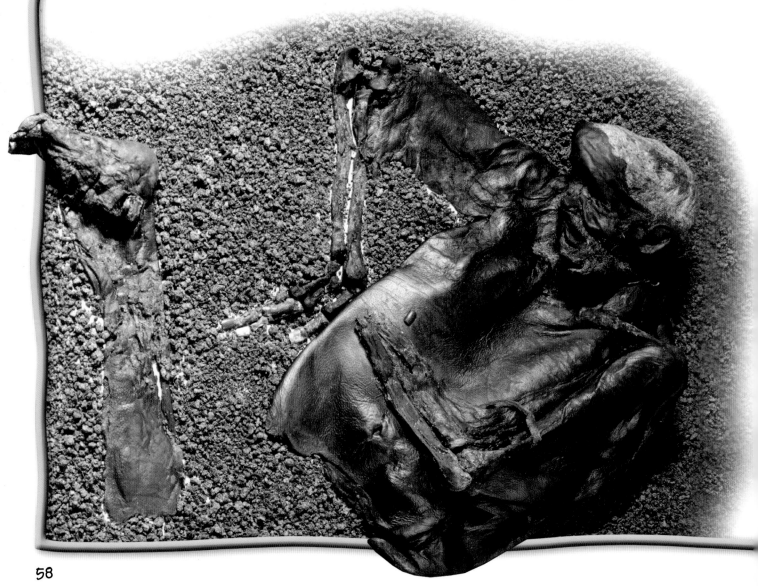

120 Lindow Man did not die peacefully. Before he died, he ate food with poisonous mistletoe in it. It's impossible to say if the poison was put there on purpose, or by accident. The marks on his body tell the story of his last moments alive. Someone hit him hard on the head, a cord was tightened around his neck and he was strangled. Then, to make sure he was dead, his throat was cut.

121 It took four years to find most of Lindow Man's body. The machine used to cut the peat had sliced it into pieces, which were found at different times. His top half, from the waist up, was found in 1984, and four years later his left leg turned up. His right leg is missing, possibly still buried in the peat bog.

▲ In this reconstruction, Lindow Man eats a meal containing burnt bread. This may have been part of a ceremony in which he was sacrificed to the gods.

I DON'T BELIEVE IT!

Visitors to the British Museum have come up with names for Lindow Man, including Sludge Man and Man in the Toilet!

122 In Lindow Man's time, gifts were given to the gods. The greatest gift was a human sacrifice, which is what may have happened to Lindow Man. After eating a meal mixed with mistletoe, he was killed and put in a bog. People thought he was leaving this world and entering the world of the gods.

Mummies of ancient Egypt

123 The most famous mummies were made in ancient Egypt. The Egyptians were skilled embalmers (mummy-makers). Pharaohs (rulers of Egypt) and ordinary people were made into mummies, along with many kinds of animal.

▲ Even pet dogs were mummified in ancient Egypt.

▲ Two people walk through the Field of Reeds, which was the ancient Egyptian name for paradise.

124 Mummies were made because the Egyptians thought that the dead needed their bodies in a new life after death. They believed a person would live forever in paradise, but only if their body was saved. Every Egyptian wanted to travel to paradise after death. This is why they went to such trouble to preserve the bodies of the dead.

125 Ancient Egypt's first mummies were made by nature. When a person died, their body was buried in a pit in the desert sand. The person was buried with objects to use in the next life. Because the sand was hot and dry, the flesh did not rot. Instead, the flesh and skin dried and shrivelled until they were stretched over the bones. The body had been mummified. Egypt's natural mummies date from around 3500 BC.

126 The ancient Egyptians made their first artificial mummies around **3400 BC.** The last mummies were made around AD 400. This means the Egyptians were making mummies for 4000 years! They stopped making them because as the Christian religion spread to Egypt, mummy-making came to be seen as a pagan (non-Christian) practice.

◀ This man died 5200 years ago in Egypt. His body slowly dried out in the hot, desert conditions, and became a natural mummy.

127 When an old grave was found, perhaps by robbers who wanted to steal the grave goods, they got a surprise. Instead of digging up a skeleton, they uncovered a dried-up body that still looked like a person! This might have started the ancient Egyptians thinking – could they find a way to preserve bodies themselves?

▶ Many Egyptian coffins were shaped like a person and beautifully painted and decorated.

Egypt's first mummy

128 The Egyptians told a myth about how the very first mummy was made. The story was about Osiris, who was ruler of Egypt. It explained how Osiris became the first mummy, and because it had happened to him, people wanted to follow his example and be mummified when they died.

129 The story begins with the murder of Osiris. He had a wicked brother called Seth, and one day Seth tricked Osiris into lying inside a box. The box was really a coffin. Seth shut the lid and threw the coffin into the river Nile, and Osiris drowned. Seth killed his brother because he was jealous of him – he felt the people of Egypt did not love him as much as they loved Osiris.

130 Isis was married to Osiris, and she could not bear to be parted from him. She searched throughout Egypt for his body, and when she found it, she brought it home. Isis knew that Seth would be angry if he found out what she had done, and so she hid the dead body of Osiris.

▶ Isis, Anubis and Thoth rebuild the body of Osiris to make the first mummy.

QUIZ

1. Who killed Osiris?
2. Who was the wife of Osiris?
3. How many pieces did Seth cut Osiris into?
4. Which three gods helped Isis?
5. What did Osiris become in the afterlife?

Answers:
1. Seth 2. Isis 3. 14
4. Ra, Anubis, Thoth
5. King of the dead

131 **However Seth found out, and he took the body of Osiris from its hiding place.** Seth cut Osiris into 14 pieces, which he scattered far and wide across Egypt. At last, he thought, he had finally got rid of Osiris.

132 **Seth might have destroyed Osiris, but he could not destroy the love that Isis had for him.** Once again, Isis searched for Osiris. She turned herself into a kite (a bird of prey), and flew high above Egypt so she could look down upon the land to see where Seth had hidden the body parts of Osiris. One by one, Isis found the pieces of her husband's body, except for one, which was eaten by a fish.

133 **Isis brought the pieces together.** She wept at the sight of her husband's body. When Ra, the sun god, saw her tears, he sent the gods Anubis and Thoth to help her. Anubis wrapped the pieces of Osiris' body in cloth. Then Isis, Anubis and Thoth laid them out in the shape of Osiris and wrapped the whole body. The first mummy had been made. Isis kissed the mummy and Osiris was reborn, not to live in this world, but to live forever in the afterlife as king of the dead.

A very messy job

134 Mummies were made in Egypt for almost 4000 years. Mummy-makers experimented with different methods of preserving the dead, some of which worked better than others. The best mummies were made during a time of Egyptian history called the New Kingdom, between 3550 and 3069 years ago.

135 A Greek called Herodotus wrote down one way the Egyptians made mummies. Herodotus visited Egypt in the 400s BC. He was told it took 70 days to make a mummy – 15 days to cleanse the body, 40 days to dry it out, and 15 days to wrap it.

136 Mummy-makers worked in open-air tents. Their simple workshops, which were far from villages and towns, were along the west bank of the river Nile. The tents were left open so that bad smells were carried away on the breeze. They were near the river as water was needed in the mummy-making process.

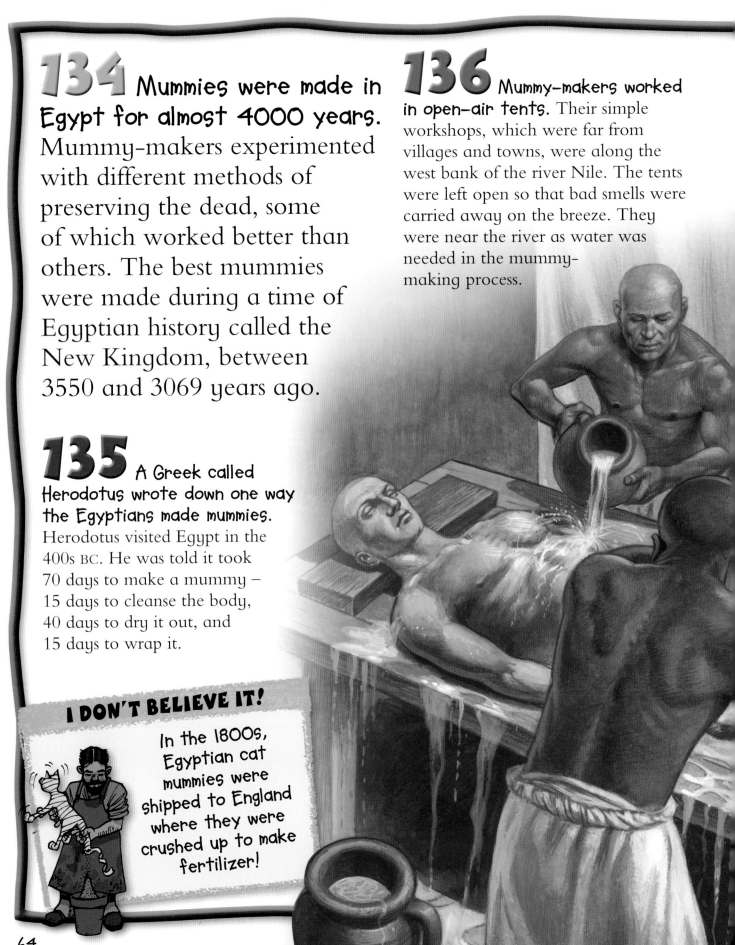

I DON'T BELIEVE IT!

In the 1800s, Egyptian cat mummies were shipped to England where they were crushed up to make fertilizer!

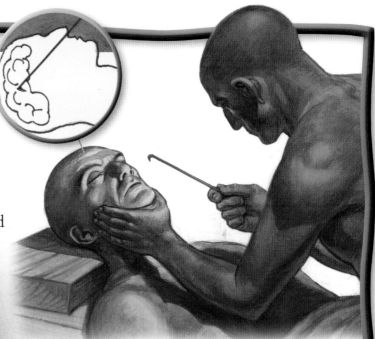

▶ To remove the brain, a metal hook was pushed up through the left nostril. It was then used to pull the brain out through the nose.

137 Mummy-making skills were handed down from one generation to the next. It was a job for men only, and it was a father's duty to train his son. A boy learned by watching his father at work. If his father worked as a slitter – the man who made the first cut in the body – his son also became a slitter.

138 The first 15 days of making a mummy involved cleaning the body. In the Place of Purification tent, the body was washed with salty water. It was then taken to the House of Beauty tent. Here, the brain was removed and thrown away. Then a slit was made in the left side of the body and the liver, lungs, intestines and stomach were taken out and kept.

139 The heart was left inside the body. The Egyptians thought the heart was the centre of intelligence. They believed it was needed to guide the person in the next life. If the heart was removed by mistake, it was put back inside. The kidneys were also left inside the body.

◀ A dead body was carefully washed with salty water before its organs were removed.

Drying the body

140 After the insides had been taken out, the body was dried. Mummy-makers used a special salt called natron to do the drying. The salt was a powdery-white mixture and was found along the edges of lakes in the north of Egypt. The natron was put into baskets, then taken to the mummy-makers.

143 The liver, lungs, intestines and stomach were also dried. Each of these organs was placed in a separate pottery bowl, and natron was piled on top. Just like the body, these organs were also left for 40 days, during which time the natron dried them out.

Bags of natron

141 At the workshop, small linen bags were filled with natron. The bags were packed into the empty body through the slit where the insides had been taken out. As well as the natron, rags, straw, dried grass and sawdust were also stuffed into the body. They helped to give the body its human shape.

Dried grass

Sawdust

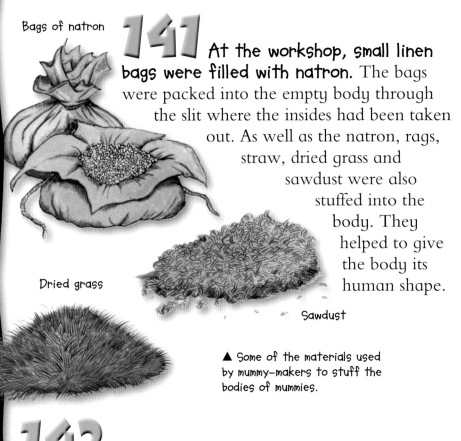

▲ Some of the materials used by mummy-makers to stuff the bodies of mummies.

142 Next, the body was placed on its back on a table and covered in a thick layer of natron. No flesh was left exposed. The body was left to dry out under the natron for 40 days.

144

Fisherman first used natron to dry the fish they caught. They realized that natron's salty crystals sucked juices out of dead flesh, leaving it dry. Dried, or salted, fish did not rot. This was why the mummy-makers began to use natron to preserve the dead.

145

During the 40 days of drying, the natron absorbed the body's juices. At the end of this time, the mummy-makers scraped away the natron and removed the materials used to stuff the body. The dried body had lost about three-quarters of its original weight and was shrivelled, hard and blue-black in colour. It hardly looked like a body at all.

▲ The body was covered in natron, a kind of salt, to dry it out. Up to 225 kilograms were needed.

Wrapped from head to toe

146 **The next job was to make the body appear lifelike.** The body cavity was filled and the skin was rubbed with oil and spices to make it soft and sweet-smelling. Then it was given false eyes and a wig, and make-up was applied. Lastly, tree resin was poured over it. This set into a hard layer to stop mould growing.

147 **The dried-out organs were wrapped in linen, then put into containers called canopic jars.** The container with the baboon head (the god Hapi) held the lungs, and the stomach was put into the jackal-headed jar (the god Duamutef). The human-headed jar (the god Imseti) protected the liver, and the intestines were placed in the falcon-headed jar (the god Qebehsenuef).

148 **The cut on the left side of the body was rarely stitched up.** Instead, it was covered with a wax plaque. On the plaque was a design known as the Eye of Horus. The Egyptians believed it had the power to see evil and stop it from entering the body through the cut.

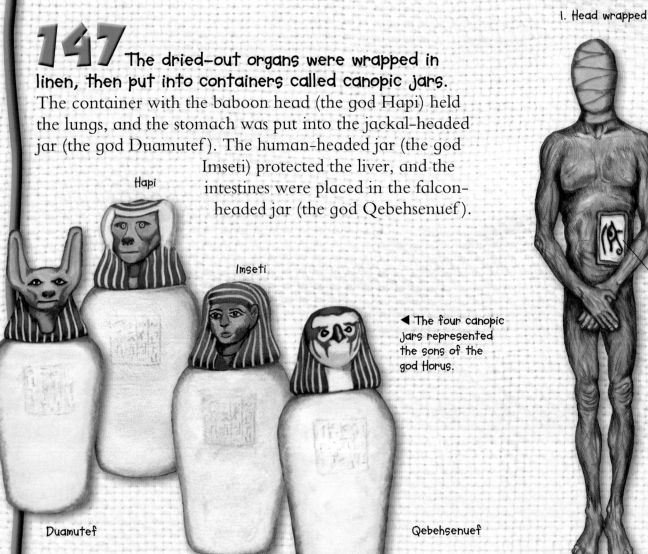

Hapi

Imseti

◄ The four canopic jars represented the sons of the god Horus.

Duamutef

Qebehsenuef

1. Head wrapped

Eye of Horus

149

In the final part of the process, the body was wrapped. It took 11 days to do this. The body was wrapped in strips of linen, 6 to 20 centimetres wide. There was a set way of wrapping the body, which always started with the head. Lastly, the body was covered with a sheet of linen, tied with linen bands.

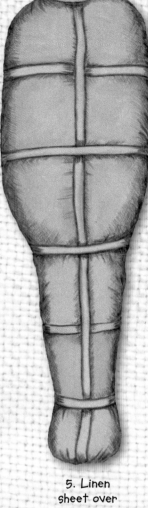

5. Linen sheet over wrappings

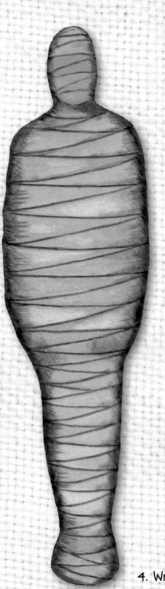

4. Wrapping complete

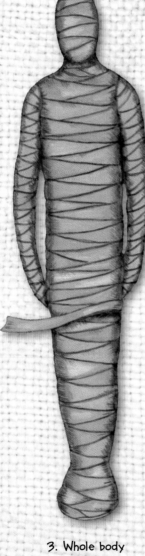

3. Whole body wrapped

▲ There was a five-stage sequence for wrapping the body, which always started with the head.

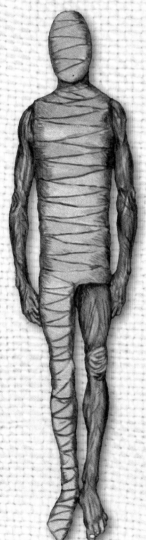

2. Limbs and torso wrapped

150

During the wrapping, amulets (lucky charms) were placed between the layers of linen. These protected the person from harm on their journey to the afterlife. Magic spells written on the wrappings were another form of protection. After wrapping, resin was poured over the mummy to make it waterproof. Last, it was given a face mask.

Tombs and tomb robbers

151 The body was placed in a wooden coffin. Simple coffins were made from planks of wood, and expensive ones were shaped like a person. They were decorated with spells. A picture on the inside of the coffin showed the route to the afterlife.

152 The earliest pharaohs were buried in pyramid tombs. The first pyramid was built about 2650 BC, for Pharaoh Djoser. For the next 800 years, all pharaohs were buried in pyramids. However robbers found their way into all of them. Later pharaohs were buried in tombs cut into a rocky valley, known as the Valley of the Kings. Robbers found many of these tombs too, but not all.

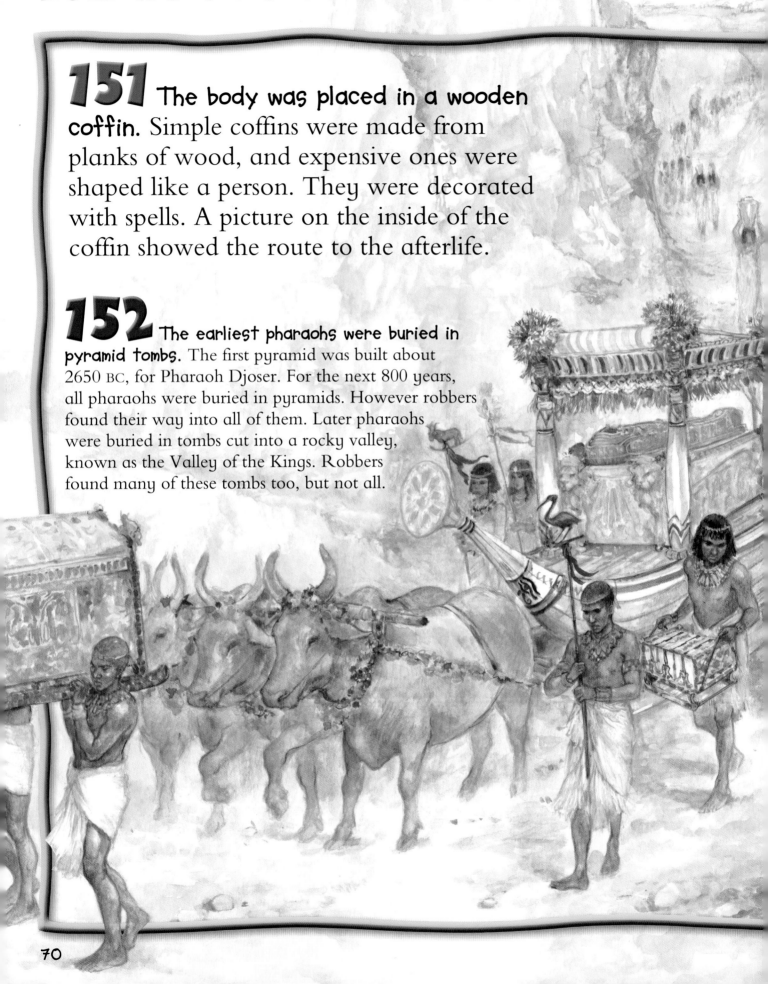

153 On the day of burial, the mummy was lifted out of its coffin and stood upright. A priest used a Y-shaped stone tool to touch the mummy's mouth, eyes, nose and ears. This was the Opening of the Mouth ceremony. It was done so that the person's speech, sight, hearing and smell came back to them for use in the next life.

▲ A priest (right) about to touch a mummy (left) in the Opening of the Mouth ceremony.

154 Mummies were buried with grave goods. These were items for the person to use in the next life. Ordinary people were buried with basic items, such as food and drink. Pharaohs and wealthy people were buried with everything they would need in their next life, such as furniture, clothes, weapons, jewellery and musical instruments.

155 Tombs were tempting places to robbers. They knew what was inside them, and took great risks to break in and steal the goods. Not even a mummy was safe – the tomb robbers smashed coffins open, and cut their way through the layers of linen wrappings to get at the masks, amulets and jewellery. Tomb robbery was a major crime, and if a robber was caught he was put to death.

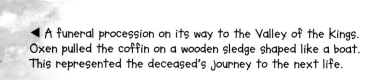

◄ A funeral procession on its way to the Valley of the Kings. Oxen pulled the coffin on a wooden sledge shaped like a boat. This represented the deceased's journey to the next life.

Tutankhamun, the boy-king

156 Tutankhamun is one of Egypt's most famous pharaohs. He became king in 1334 BC when he was eight years old. Because he was too young to carry out the important work of ruling Egypt, two of his ministers took charge. They were Ay, chief minister, and Horemheb, head of the army. They made decisions on Tutankhamun's behalf.

◀ This model of Tutankhamun was buried with him in his tomb.

157 Tutankhamun was pharaoh for about nine years. He died when he was 17 years old. His body was mummified and buried in a tomb cut into the side of a valley. Many pharaohs were laid to rest in this valley, known as the Valley of the Kings. Tutankhamun was buried with valuables for use in the next life.

158 The tombs in the Valley of the Kings were meant to be secret. However robbers found them, and stole the precious items buried there. They found Tutankhamun's tomb, but were caught before they could do much damage. Years later, when the tomb of Rameses VI was being dug, rubble rolled down the valley and blocked the entrance to Tutankhamun's tomb. After that, it was forgotten about.

◀ Tutankhamun's throne. The back is decorated with a picture of the pharaoh, who is seated, and a princess.

159
In 1922, British archaeologist Howard Carter discovered the tomb of Tutankhamun. He had spent years searching for it. Other archaeologists thought he was wasting his time. They said all the tombs in the valley had already been found. Carter refused to give up, and in November 1922 he found a stairway that led to the door of a tomb.

160
Behind the door was a corridor. At the end of it was a second door, which Carter made a hole in. He peered through the hole, and said he could see 'wonderful things'. It took ten years to remove all the objects from the tomb – jewellery and a gold throne were among the treasures. A gold mask covered the king's head and shoulders. It was made of 10 kilograms of pure gold.

▼ Tutankhamun was buried in three separate coffins that fitted inside each other. This is the middle coffin, which is made of gold and decorated with a gem called lapis lazuli.

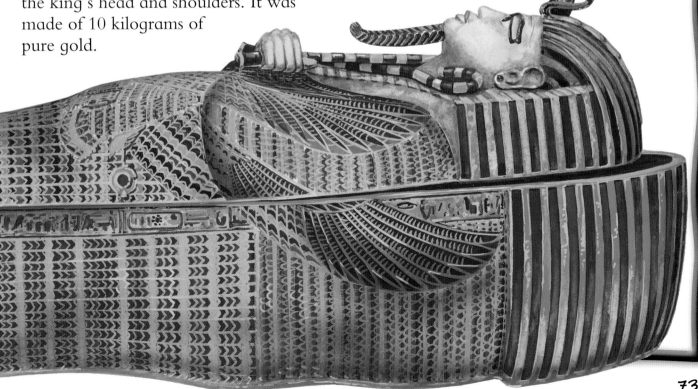

Magnificent mummies!

161 The mummy of pharaoh Rameses II was found in 1871. It had been buried in a tomb, but had been moved to prevent robbers finding it. Rameses II had bad teeth, probably caused by eating gritty bread. He was in his eighties when he died and had arthritis, which would have given him painful joints. In 1976 his mummy was sent to France for treatment to stop mould from damaging it.

162 Mummy 1770 is in the Manchester Museum, UK. This is a mummy of a teenage girl, whose real name is not known. Her lower legs and feet are missing, and the mummy-makers had given her false ones to make her appear whole. It's a mystery what happened to her, but she might have been bitten by a crocodile, or even a hippo, as she paddled in the river Nile 3000 years ago.

▼ The mummy of Rameses II. Scientific studies have shown that particularly fine linen was used to stuff and bandage the body.

163

A trapped donkey led to the discovery of thousands of mummies! It happened in 1996, when a donkey slipped into a hole at Egypt's Bahariya Oasis. The owner freed it, then climbed down into an underground system of chambers lined with thousands of mummies of ordinary people. The site is called the Valley of the Golden Mummies, as many of the mummies have golden masks over their faces. They are about 2000 years old.

164

Djedmaatesankh – Djed for short – is an Egyptian mummy in the Royal Ontario Museum, Toronto, Canada. She lived around 850 BC, and in 1977 she entered the history books as the first Egyptian mummy to have a whole-body CAT scan (computerized axial tomography). The CAT images revealed that Djed had a serious infection in her jaw, which may have caused her death.

QUIZ

1. What was damaging Rameses II?

2. What is false about Mummy 1770?

3. What did a donkey help to find?

4. Which mummy had the first CAT scan?

Answers:
1. Mould 2. Her legs and feet 3. The Valley of the Golden Mummies 4. Djed

Mummies of Peru

165 **Mummies were made in Peru, South America, for hundreds of years.** The first were made in the 400s BC, and the last probably in the early 1500s AD. A body was put into a sitting position, with its knees tucked under its chin. Layers of cloth were wrapped around it to make a 'mummy bundle'. The body was preserved by the dry, cold environment.

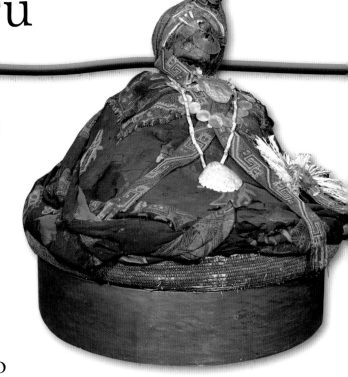

▲ This mummy from Peru is more than 500 years old. It was covered in cloth to make a 'mummy bundle'.

▲ Mummies of emperors were carried through the streets and put on display to the public.

166 **In the 1500s, the mummies of Inca emperors were paraded through the streets of Cuzco, Peru.** People thought that by doing this the souls of the dead were well-cared for, and this helped them on their journey into the afterlife. People also believed that this practice pleased the gods, who then ensured that living people were healthy and happy.

I DON'T BELIEVE IT!
When Spaniards came to Peru in the 1500s, they destroyed thousands of Inca mummies – they got rid of 1365 in just four years!

167

The Incas sacrificed children to their gods.
They hoped that in return the gods would provide rain for
crops, good health and prosperity. The children's bodies
were left at the tops of freezing mountains, where they
slowly turned into natural mummies.

168

**In 1995,
the mummy of a
teenage Inca girl was
found.** She was led to
her death 500 years
ago, as a sacrifice to
the gods. Her body was
left 6300 metres up
Mount Ampato, Peru,
with offerings of cloth,
food, gold and silver. The
icy conditions preserved
her body.

▶ Inca children stand in front of a priest
as they prepare to be sacrificed to the
gods in a religious ceremony.

Mummies from Asia

169 More than 2500 years ago, the Pazyryk people of Siberia, Russia, buried their leaders in the region's frozen ground. In 1993, a Pazyryk burial mound was dug up, and inside was the frozen mummy of the 'Ice Princess'. She was dressed in clothes made from silk and wool, and she wore a pair of riding boots. When her body thawed from the ice, pictures of deer were found tattooed on her skin.

▲ The Pazyryk people tattooed images of snow leopards, eagles and reindeer onto their bodies. Those found on the 'Ice Princess' may have been a mark of her importance, or rank.

170 Lady Ch'eng is one of the world's best-preserved mummies. She was found in China, and is 2100 years old. Her body had been placed inside a coffin filled with a strange liquid that contained mercury (a silvery liquid metal, also known as quicksilver). The coffin was sealed and placed inside another, and then another. The coffins were buried under a mound of charcoal and clay, and in this watertight, airtight tomb her body was preserved.

◀ This artist's impression shows how Lady Ch'eng may have looked when she was alive more than 2000 years ago.

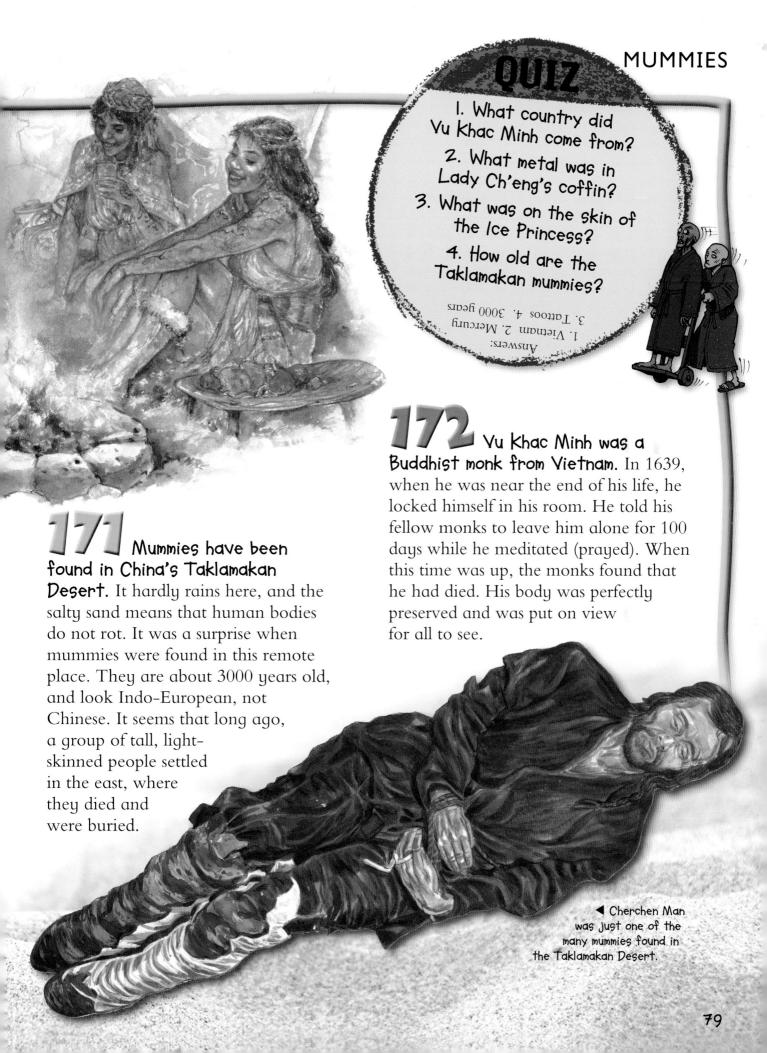

QUIZ

1. What country did Vu Khac Minh come from?

2. What metal was in Lady Ch'eng's coffin?

3. What was on the skin of the Ice Princess?

4. How old are the Taklamakan mummies?

Answers:
1. Vietnam 2. Mercury 3. Tattoos 4. 3000 years

171 Mummies have been found in China's Taklamakan Desert. It hardly rains here, and the salty sand means that human bodies do not rot. It was a surprise when mummies were found in this remote place. They are about 3000 years old, and look Indo-European, not Chinese. It seems that long ago, a group of tall, light-skinned people settled in the east, where they died and were buried.

172 Vu Khac Minh was a Buddhist monk from Vietnam. In 1639, when he was near the end of his life, he locked himself in his room. He told his fellow monks to leave him alone for 100 days while he meditated (prayed). When this time was up, the monks found that he had died. His body was perfectly preserved and was put on view for all to see.

◀ Cherchen Man was just one of the many mummies found in the Taklamakan Desert.

North American mummies

173 At 9000 years old, Spirit Cave Man is one of the oldest mummies. The mummy was found in Spirit Cave, Nevada, USA, in 1940. It was wearing a cloak of animal skins, leather moccasins on its feet, and was wrapped inside mats made of tough grass. The cool, dry air in the cave had dried the body, turning it into a natural mummy.

▲ The mummy of Spirit Cave Man. Although it was discovered in 1940, the mummy's actual age was not determined until 1994.

I DON'T BELIEVE IT!

Hazel Farris, like Elmer McCurdy, was another American outlaw whose mummified body was put on show at funfairs.

174 The mummy of the North American Iceman no longer exists. It was found in 1999, in Canada. The Iceman had died in the 1400s, and was preserved in a glacier. Native North Americans claimed that the man was their ancestor, so the mummy was handed to them. It was cremated, and the ashes buried near where the mummy had been found.

175 A mummy family was found on Greenland in 1972. The bodies of six Inuit women and two children had been placed on a rocky ledge, in about 1475. The cold conditions had preserved them, slowly freeze-drying their bodies.

▲ An Inuit mummy of a baby boy. He was killed so that he could stay with his mother in the afterlife.

176

Elmer McCurdy was an American outlaw who became a mummy! He was shot dead in 1911 after robbing a train. His body was taken to an undertakers where it was preserved, but no one claimed the body. Eventually, McCurdy's mummy was sold to a fairground. In 1976, a TV programme was being filmed at a ghost ride, and a 'dummy' turned out to be the mummy of Elmer McCurdy! He was finally buried in 1977.

177

The mummies of three British sailors lie in the frozen ground of the Arctic. They are John Torrington, John Hartnell and William Braine, who died in 1845 during a voyage from England to find a sea route across the Arctic Ocean. Their bodies were examined in 1984, and it was discovered that they had suffered from lead poisoning, caused by eating contaminated food. The sailors were reburied, and the Arctic began to freeze their bodies again.

▼ The crew of *HMS Terror* try to dig their ship out of the Arctic ice. The men eventually died, and some of their remains were mummified in the freezing conditions.

Worldwide mummies

178 Mount Vesuvius is a volcano in southern Italy. It erupted in AD 79, and the town of Pompeii was buried under a layer of ash and rock. Many people died, mostly by suffocation. As scientists uncovered the town, they found body-shaped areas in the ground. By pouring plaster of Paris into the areas, the shapes of the dead were revealed.

▲ This plaster cast shows a victim of the Vesuvius eruption in AD 79. Some of the casts are so detailed, even facial expressions can be seen.

▼ Fully-dressed mummies line the walls of a church in Palermo, Italy. The dead wished to be preserved wearing their finest clothes.

179 In the underground crypt of a church in Palermo, Sicily, are more than 2000 human mummies. These are the bodies of local people, who were buried more than 100 years ago. Instead of rotting away, the dry air has mummified their remains. Many of the mummies are propped against the walls, where they stand at odd angles, dressed in burial clothes.

180
The mummies of saints are displayed in many Roman Catholic churches. It isn't always the whole body that is on show, sometimes it is just a body part, called a 'relic'. Many of the mummies are natural, and are the result of being in a dry environment for many years. A few are artificial, and have been preserved on purpose. However, the Catholic Church believes that some saints have been preserved by God, and are evidence of miracles.

▲ The body of Saint Bernadette Soubirous (1844–1879) at Lourdes, France. Her body was exhumed (dug up) from her grave three times, and had not decomposed. People believed that she had been preserved by God.

182
In Japan, there are about 20 mummies of Buddhist priests. The mummy of Tetsumonkai is one of them. He died in 1829, and a few years before his death he started to prepare his body for mummification. He ate less, and stopped eating rice, barley, wheat, beans and millet, as he believed that they harmed the body. After he died, his fellow priests put him in a sitting position with his legs crossed, and then dried out his body.

◀ The mummy of Tetsumonkai. His fellow priests dried his body by placing burning candles around it.

181
Mummies have been made on the island of Papua New Guinea for generations. When a person died, they were put into a squatting position and their body was left to dry in the sun, or smoke-dried over a fire. Because the body was preserved, islanders believed their dead relatives were still living with them.

Studying mummies

183 Until recently, mummies were studied by opening them up. Unwrapping Egyptian mummies was popular in the 1800s, and was often done in front of an audience. Thomas Pettigrew (1791–1865) was an English surgeon who unwrapped many mummies at this time. He wrote some of the finest books about Egyptian mummies.

▲ An audience looks on as a mummy is unwrapped in the 1800s. This process destroyed lots of historical evidence.

184 There is no need to open up mummies today. Instead, mummies are studied by taking X-rays of bones, while scans reveal soft tissue in great detail. Mummies can even be tested to work out which families they came from.

▼ A Polish scientist prepares a 3000-year-old Egyptian mummy for an X-ray.

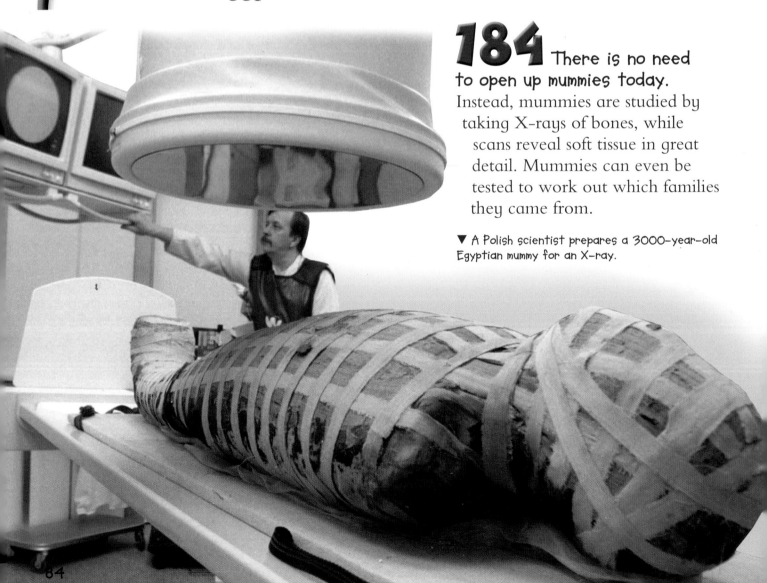

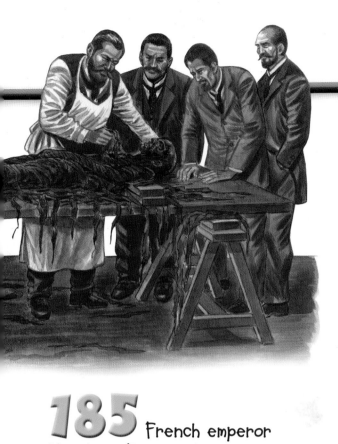

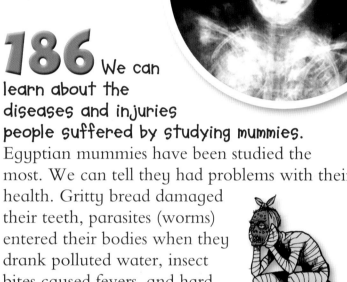

► This X-ray of a mummy's skull reveals that a fractured skull was the cause of death.

186 We can learn about the diseases and injuries people suffered by studying mummies. Egyptian mummies have been studied the most. We can tell they had problems with their health. Gritty bread damaged their teeth, parasites (worms) entered their bodies when they drank polluted water, insect bites caused fevers, and hard work led to problems with their joints and bones.

185 French emperor Napoleon Bonaparte was fascinated by mummies. After defeating the British in 1798, Napoleon and his troops became stranded in Egypt. With Napoleon were 150 scientists, who began to study Egypt and its mummies.

▼ When Napoleon left Egypt in 1799, he left behind a team of historians and scientists to study Egypt for him.

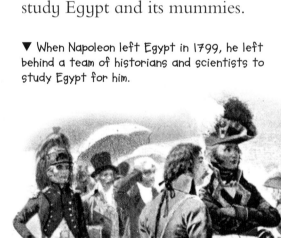

Animal mummies

187 **Animals were mummified in ancient Egypt, too!** Birds and fish were mummified as food for a dead person in the next life. Pet cats, dogs and monkeys became mummies so they could keep their dead owners company. Some bulls were believed to be holy as it was thought the spirits of the gods lived inside them. When they died, the bulls were mummified and buried underground.

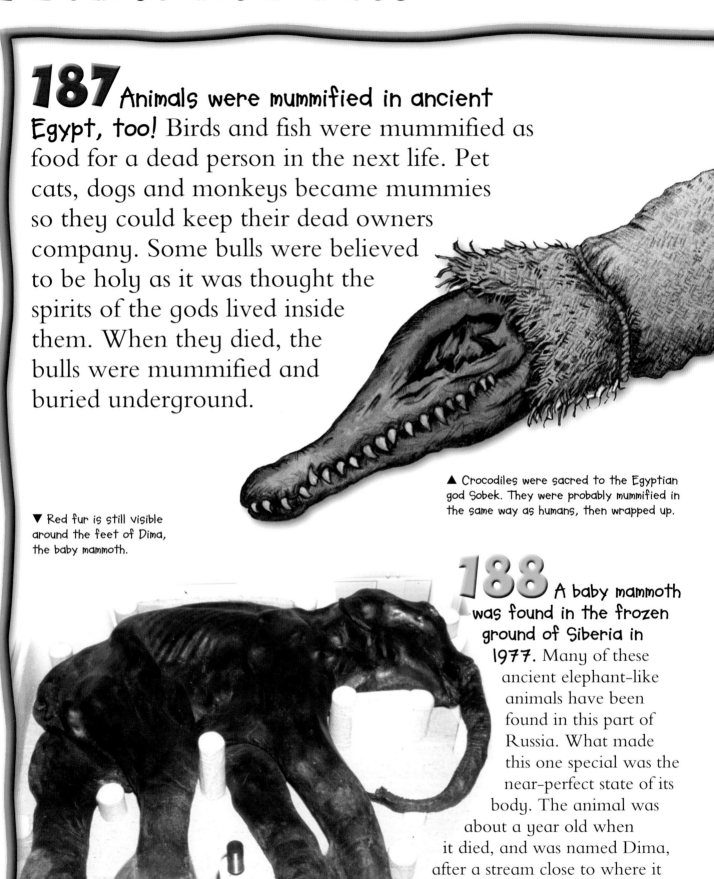

▲ Crocodiles were sacred to the Egyptian god Sobek. They were probably mummified in the same way as humans, then wrapped up.

▼ Red fur is still visible around the feet of Dima, the baby mammoth.

188 **A baby mammoth was found in the frozen ground of Siberia in 1977.** Many of these ancient elephant-like animals have been found in this part of Russia. What made this one special was the near-perfect state of its body. The animal was about a year old when it died, and was named Dima, after a stream close to where it was discovered.

189 **The world's oldest mummy is a dinosaur!** It is the fossil of an *Edmontosaurus*, which was found in Wyoming, USA, in 1908. This dinosaur died 65 million years ago, but instead of becoming a skeleton, its body was baked dry by the sun. When US fossil hunter Charles Sternberg discovered it, the skin and insides had been fossilized, as well as the bones.

▲ This frog was naturally mummified in 2006 when it died in a plant pot. The sun baked it dry.

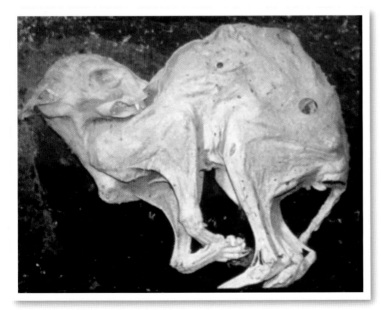

▲ This mummified cat was found in 1971 in Sudbury, Suffolk, UK. It had been walled up in an old mill to protect the building from harm.

190 **Cats have been made into mummies for thousands of years.** In ancient Egypt, cats were linked to the goddess, Bastet. They were bred to be killed as religious offerings at temples. Cat mummies are sometimes found behind the walls of old houses in Europe. It was believed a cat could bring good fortune, so a cat's body was sometimes walled up, after which it dried out to become a mummy.

Mummy stories

191 The idea of the 'mummy's curse' started in 1923. A letter printed by a London newspaper said people would be cursed if they disturbed any pharaoh's tomb. Tutankhamun's tomb had just been found and people seemed to believe in curses. The letter seemed to confirm their fears. In fact, the entire thing was all made up!

▼ The opening of Tutankhamun's tomb by Howard Carter was the basis for the 'curse of the mummy'.

192 Mummies have not been used to make newspaper! There's a story that says linen was stripped from the mummies of Egypt, then used to make paper. The story goes on to say that an American newspaper was printed on this so-called 'mummy paper', sometime in the 1800s. It's a great story, but not true!

193

A mummy didn't sink Titanic in 1912! In the British Museum, London, is the lid of an Egyptian coffin. It is known as the 'Unlucky Mummy' as it's thought to be cursed. English journalist William Stead was on board *Titanic* when it sank. He told a story about the 'Unlucky Mummy' on the night the ship sank, and some people believed that this cursed the voyage.

▼ The 2001 film *The Mummy Returns* used lots of creepy special effects.

▼ A scene from the 1932 film *The Mummy*. Boris Karloff played the part of the mummy character, Im-Ho-Tep (left).

194

Mummies have become film stars. The first mummy film was made in 1909 and was called *The Mummy of King Rameses*. It was a black-and-white film without any sound. Many mummy films have been made since. One of the creepiest was *The Mummy*. It was made in 1932, and starred Boris Karloff.

195

As long ago as 1827, a book was written about a mummy. *The Mummy! A Tale of the Twenty-second Century* was written by Jane Loudon. The book was a science fiction story set in the year 2126. Lots more stories have been written about mummies since then – some for children. The author Jacqueline Wilson has even written *The Cat Mummy*, about a girl who tries to mummify her dead cat!

QUIZ

1. Was there a mummy on board Titanic?
2. Which mummy film did Boris Karloff star in?
3. What started in 1923?
4. Who wrote The Cat Mummy?

Answers:
1. No 2. *The Mummy*
3. The mummy's curse
4. Jacqueline Wilson

Modern-day mummies

196 In Moscow, Russia, and in Beijing, China, modern-day mummies can be found. When Vladimir Ilich Lenin died in 1924, his body was mummified and put on display in Moscow. The same thing happened in China in 1976, when Mao Zedong died. Both men were leaders of their countries, and after they died, their bodies were preserved so that people could continue to see them.

▲ The mummy of Lenin is still on display in Moscow, Russia. The body was preserved using a secret technique.

197 The wife of a leader was also mummified. Eva Perón was the wife of the president of Argentina. After her death in 1952, her body was preserved. Then in 1955 the Argentine government was overthrown, and Eva's mummy sent to Europe. It was returned to Argentina in 1974 to be buried.

I DON'T BELIEVE IT!
When the British artist Edward Burne-Jones found out that his paint was made from mummy remains, he buried the tube, and put daisies on the 'grave'!

198 An old man was mummified in America in 1994. A team of experts became the first people in modern times to mummify a human using ancient Egyptian techniques. They used the same tools as those used by the Egyptian mummy-makers. Then the organs were removed, the body was dried with natron and wrapped in linen.

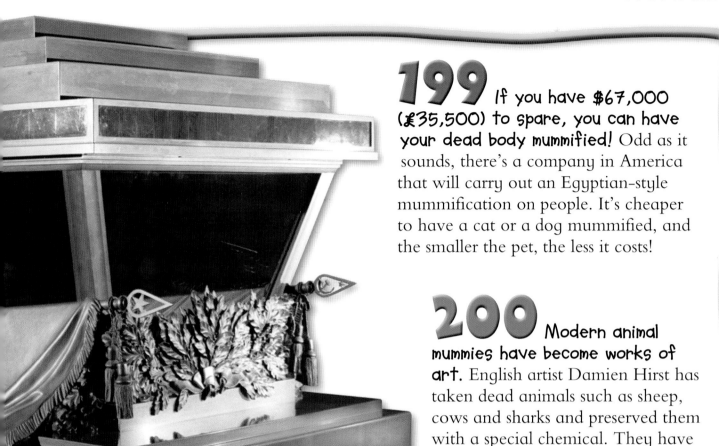

199 If you have $67,000 (£35,500) to spare, you can have your dead body mummified! Odd as it sounds, there's a company in America that will carry out an Egyptian-style mummification on people. It's cheaper to have a cat or a dog mummified, and the smaller the pet, the less it costs!

200 Modern animal mummies have become works of art. English artist Damien Hirst has taken dead animals such as sheep, cows and sharks and preserved them with a special chemical. They have then been displayed to the public in art galleries as works of art.

▼ This preserved sheep was put on display in London by Damien Hirst in 1994.

ANCIENT GREECE

201 **Ancient Greece was a small country, but its people had great ideas.** From around 2000 BC, they created a splendid civilization that reached its peak between 500–400 BC. All citizens contributed to a society that respected people's rights, encouraged the best in human nature and lived in harmony with the natural world. Today, we still admire Greek sport, medicine, drama, politics, poetry and art.

▲ The agora (town square) of Athens was a meeting place for citizens and an open–air market. Traders sold fresh fruit and vegetables and craftworkers sold cloth and pottery.

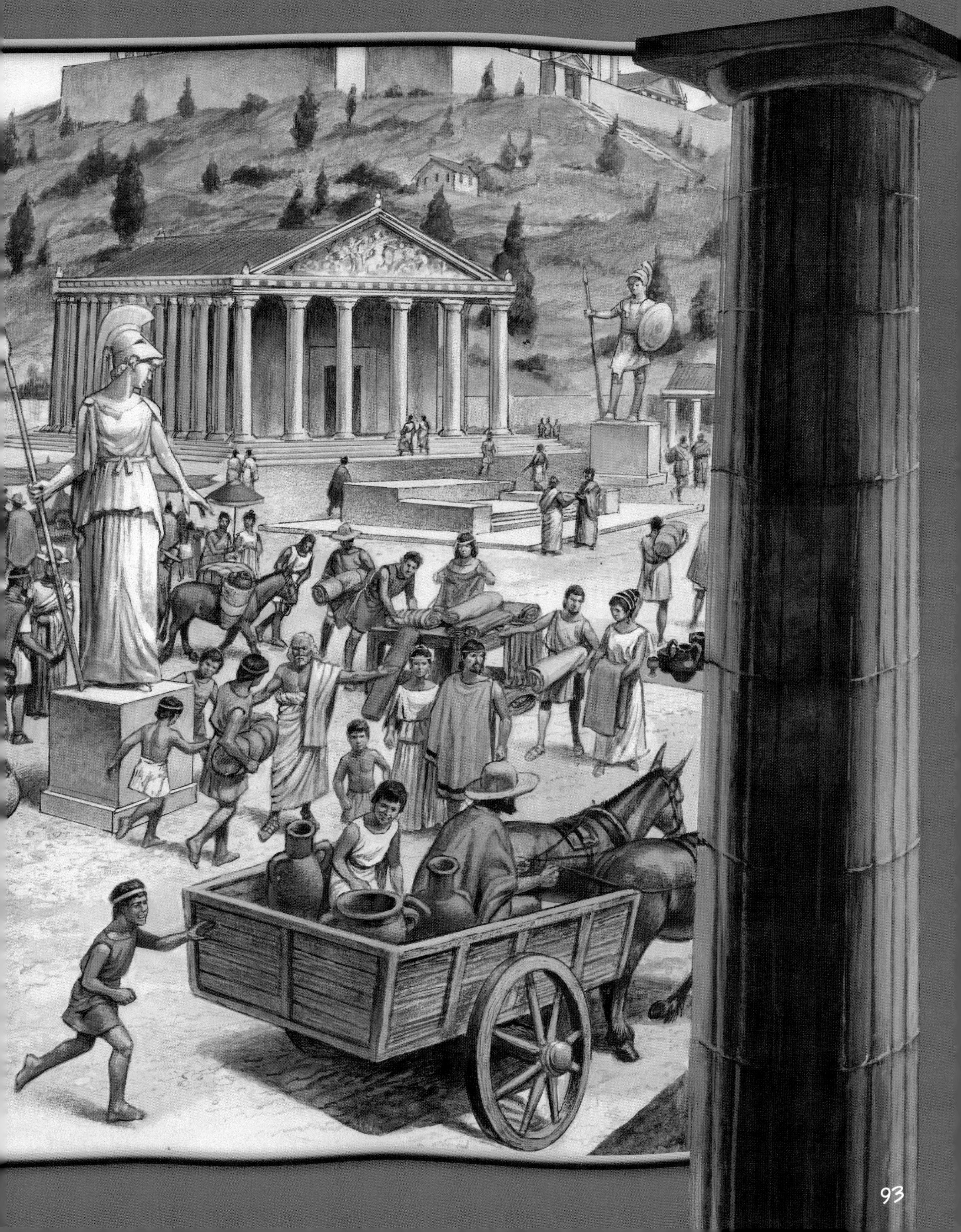

Greek homelands

202 **The Greeks thought that they were better than other people.** They saw all foreigners as uncivilized 'barbarians' who did not share the same values and beliefs, or follow the Greeks' lifestyle. Even worse, they did not speak or understand the elegant Greek language.

203 **Lifestyle was shaped by the seasons.** Winters were cold with icy winds, pouring rain and storms. Summers were very hot and dry with droughts, dust and forest fires. Spring was green and fresh – a time to plant crops and fight wars. Autumn with its harvest of ripe olives, grapes and grain was the busiest time for farmers.

▼ Neat rows of olive trees growing on a Greek farm. Olives were mixed with salt then stored in jars to eat, or crushed to make oil.

▼ The Greeks' homeland included mainland Greece and over 2000 islands in the Aegean Sea and the Ionian Sea, together with the coast of Asia Minor.

THRACE

MACEDONIA

Mount Olympus

GREECE

IONIAN SEA

Olympia

Athens

Sparta

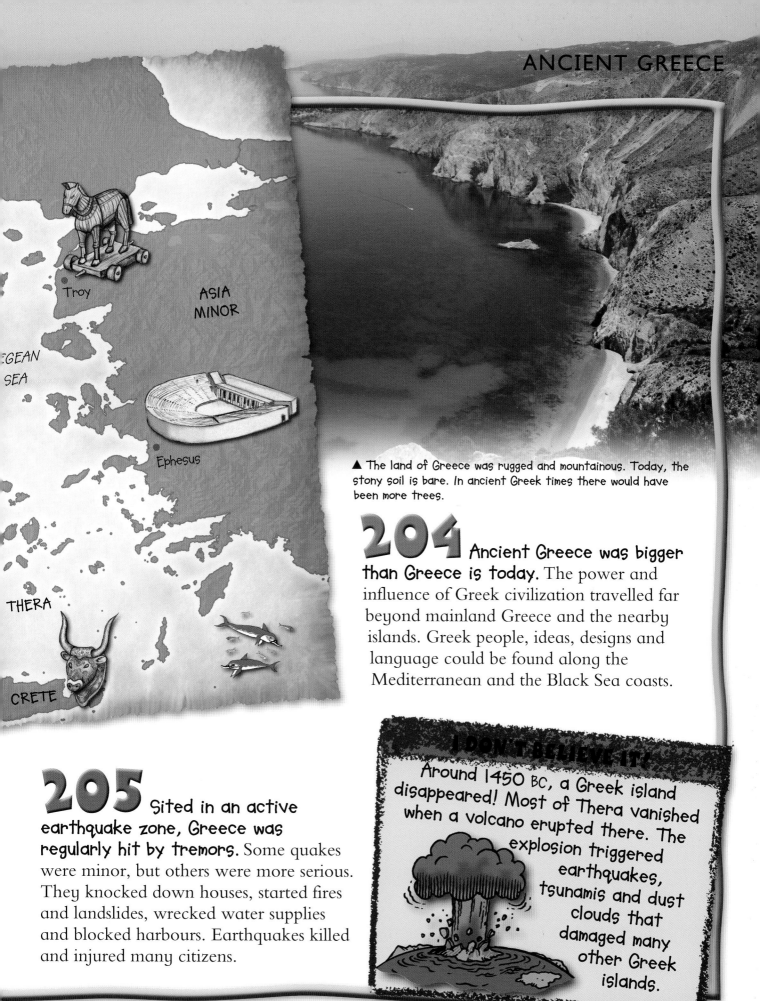

Troy

ASIA MINOR

Ephesus

EGEAN SEA

THERA

CRETE

▲ The land of Greece was rugged and mountainous. Today, the stony soil is bare. In ancient Greek times there would have been more trees.

204 **Ancient Greece was bigger than Greece is today.** The power and influence of Greek civilization travelled far beyond mainland Greece and the nearby islands. Greek people, ideas, designs and language could be found along the Mediterranean and the Black Sea coasts.

205 Sited in an active earthquake zone, Greece was regularly hit by tremors. Some quakes were minor, but others were more serious. They knocked down houses, started fires and landslides, wrecked water supplies and blocked harbours. Earthquakes killed and injured many citizens.

I DON'T BELIEVE IT!
Around 1450 BC, a Greek island disappeared! Most of Thera vanished when a volcano erupted there. The explosion triggered earthquakes, tsunamis and dust clouds that damaged many other Greek islands.

Steeped in history

206 **The ancient Greeks were proud of their beautiful country.** There were high snowy mountains, swift rushing streams, thick forests, flowery meadows and narrow, fertile plains beside the sea. Around the coast there were thousands of rocky islands, some small and poor, others large and prosperous.

◄ A carved stone figure of a woman found in the Cyclades Islands. The design is very simple but strong and graceful.

▼ This timeline shows some of the important events in the history of ancient Greece.

207 **Greek civilization began on the islands.** Some of the first evidence of farming in Greece comes from the Cyclades Islands. Around 6000 BC, people living there began to plant grain and build villages. They buried their dead in graves filled with treasures, such as carved marble figures, pottery painted with magic sun symbols and gold and silver jewellery.

TIMELINE OF GREECE

c. 40,000 BC
First people in Greece. They are hunters and gatherers

c. 2000–1450 BC
Minoan civilization on the island of Crete

c. 1250 BC
Traditional date of the Trojan War

c. 900–700 BC
Greek civilization grows strong again

c. 6000 BC
First farmers in Greece

c. 1600–1100 BC
Mycenean civilization on mainland Greece

c. 1100–900 BC
A time of decline – kingdoms weaken, writing stops

c. 776 BC
Traditional date of first Olympic Games

◀ This jar, made around 900 BC, is rather dull and plain. It suggests that times were troubled and Greek people had no money to spare for art.

208
Between 1100–900 BC, Greek history is a mystery. From 2000–1100 BC, powerful kings ruled Greece. They left splendid buildings and objects behind them, and used writing. But between around 1100–900 BC, there werc no strong kingdoms, little art, few new buildings, and writing disappeared.

▲ Alexander the Great conquered an empire stretching from Greece to India.

209
Migrants settled in distant lands. By around 700 BC, Greece was overcrowded. There were too many people, not enough farmland to grow food and some islands were short of water. Greek families left to set up colonies far away, from southern France to North Africa, Turkey and Bulgaria.

210
When the neighbours invaded, Greek power collapsed. After 431 BC, Greek cities were at war and the fighting weakened them. In 338 BC, Philip II of Macedonia (a kingdom north of Greece) invaded with a large army. After Philip died, his son, Alexander the Great, made Greece part of his empire.

c. 700–500 BC
Greeks set up colonies around Mediterranean Sea

c. 480–479 BC
Greece fights invaders from Persia (now Iran)

c. 338 BC
Philip II of Macedonia conquers Greece

c. 147–146 BC
Romans conquer Greece and Macedonia

c. 500–430 BC
Athens leads Greece, creates amazing art, has democratic government

c. 431–404 BC
Wars between Athens and Sparta

c. 336–323 BC
Alexander the Great of Macedonia and Greece conquers a vast empire

Kings and warriors

211 **King Minos ruled an amazing palace city.** The first great Greek civilization grew up at Knossos on the island of Crete. Historians call it 'Minoan' after its legendary king, Minos. Around 2000 BC, Minoan kings built an amazing palace-city, with rooms for 10,000 people. It was decorated with wonderful frescoes (wall paintings), statues and pottery.

▲ A section of the palace at Knossos on the island of Crete. A succession of powerful kings ruled a rich kingdom here.

212 **Minoan Greeks honoured a monster.** Greek myths describe how a fearsome monster was kept in a labyrinth (underground maze) below the palace. It was called the Minotaur, and it was half-man, half-bull.

▲ Greek legends told how the young hero Theseus bravely entered the labyrinth and killed the Minotaur.

QUIZ

1. What was the Minotaur?
2. What was the labyrinth?
3. Where was Knossos?

Answers:
1. A monster – half-man, half-bull 2. A maze underneath the Minoan royal palace 3. On the Greek island of Crete

▶ This golden mask was found in a royal tomb at Mycenae. It was made for a king who died around 1500 BC.

Oule = Hello

Khaire = Goodbye

213 **Invaders brought the Greek language.** Between around 2100–1700 BC, warriors from the north arrived in mainland Greece. They brought new words with them and their language was copied by everyone else living in Greece.

▼ Works of art found at Knossos include many images of huge, fierce bulls with athletes leaping between their horns in a deadly religious ritual.

214 **Mycenae was ruled by warrior kings.** Around 1600 BC new kings took control of Minoan lands from forts on the Greek mainland. The greatest fort was at Mycenae, in the far south of Greece. Mycenaean kings sent traders to Egypt and the Near East to exchange Greek pottery and olive oil for gold, tin and amber. They used their wealth to pay for huge tombs in which they were buried.

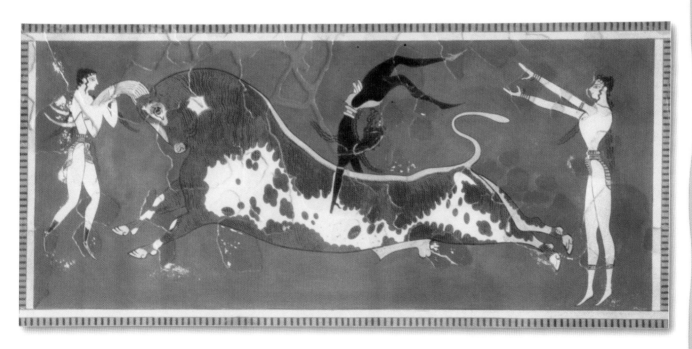

War with Troy

215 A famous Greek poem, the Iliad, describes a terrible war between the Greeks and the Trojans. The Trojans lived in a rich city on the west coast of Asia Minor (now Turkey). The Iliad was first written down around 750 BC. Ancient Greeks said the writer was a blind poet called Homer.

▼ A scene from the 2004 film *Troy*, starring Brad Pitt. The war between the Trojans and the Greeks still thrills people today. Some of the story is legend, but it may be based on real, half-remembered, facts.

MAKE HELEN'S CROWN

You will need:
gold-coloured card   ruler   scissors
sticky tape   glue   gold plastic
'jewels' or sequins   strings of beads

1. Cut a strip of gold-coloured card about 15 cm wide and 65 cm long.

2. Stick the ends of the strip together, using tape to make a circular 'crown'.

3. Decorate your crown with 'jewels' or sequins.

4. Add strings of beads hanging down at the back and the sides.

216 Queen Helen loved a Trojan prince. According to legend, the Trojan War started because Helen, the wife of Greek King Menelaus, ran away with (or was captured by) Paris, a Trojan prince. However, historians believe the main reason for the war was because the Greeks and the Trojans were rival traders.

217
The Greeks could not break through Troy's walls until they thought of a clever plan. They made a huge, hollow, wooden horse, hid warriors inside and persuaded the Trojans to accept it as an offering to the gods. The Trojans hauled the horse into their city, then the Greeks leaped out and defeated them.

218
Odysseus survived to have amazing adventures. Another famous Greek poem tells how the warrior Odysseus fought at Troy, then on the way home survived extraordinary encounters with gods, giants, witches, one-eyed monsters, sea-serpents and a man-eating whirlpool.

▶ The Cyclops was a one-eyed giant. He trapped Odysseus and his soldiers in a cave and planned to eat them. But Odysseus blinded the Cyclops, escaped from the cave and sailed away.

▶ The Iliad describes how, for ten years, the Greeks besieged the city of Troy. They eventually won the war by offering a wooden horse to the Trojans. Once inside the city walls, warriors leapt out the horse and destroyed the city.

City-states

219 The power of Mycenaean kings collapsed around 1200 BC. By 700 BC, Greece had been divided into 300 city-states, which were cities and the land around them. Some city-states were ruled by kings, some by tyrants (men who governed by force) and some by oligarchs (small groups of rich, powerful men).

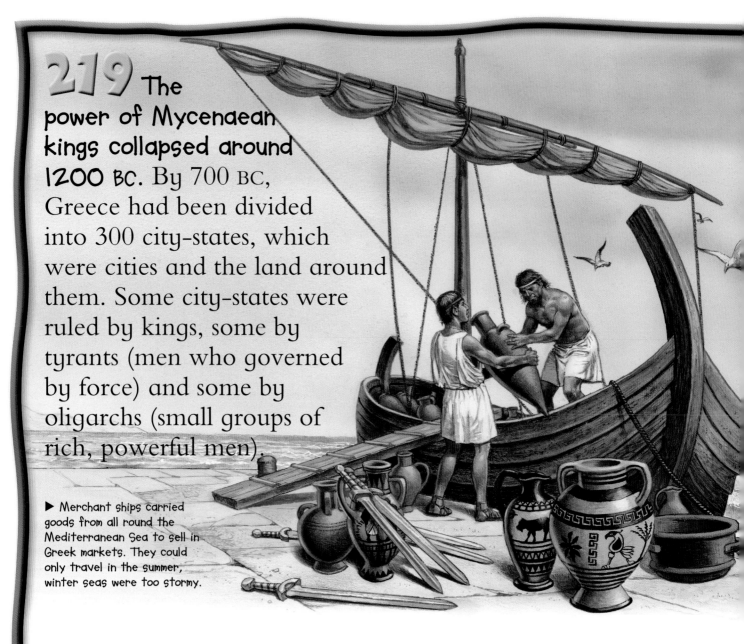

► Merchant ships carried goods from all round the Mediterranean Sea to sell in Greek markets. They could only travel in the summer, winter seas were too stormy.

220 Most city-states grew rich by buying and selling. The agora (market-place) was the centre of many cities. Goods on sale included farm produce such as grain, wine and olive oil, salt from the sea, pottery, woollen blankets, sheepskin cloaks, leather sandals and slaves.

221 Top craftsmen made fine goods for sale. Cities were home to many expert craftsmen. They ran small workshops next to their homes, or worked as slaves in factories owned by rich businessmen. Greek craftworkers were famous for producing fine pottery, stone-carvings, weapons, armour and jewellery.

222 Coins displayed city wealth and pride.

They were invented in the Near East around 600 BC. Their use soon spread to Greece, and each city state issued its own designs, stamped out of real silver. Coins were often decorated with images of gods and goddesses, heroes, monsters and favourite local animals.

▶ The design on the top coin shows the head of Alexander the Great. The other is decorated with an owl, the symbol of Athens' guardian goddess, Athena.

◀▲ The walls and gates guarding the city of Mycenae were made of huge stone slabs. The gate had a huge sculpture of two lions above it.

223 Cities were defended by strong stone walls.

City-states were proud, independent and quarrelsome. They were often at war with their rivals. They were also in constant danger of attack from neighbouring nations, especially Persia (now Iran). To protect their homes, temples, workshops, market-places and harbours, citizens built strong wooden gates and high stone walls.

▶ Many Greek ships were wrecked together with their cargoes. Some have survived on the seabed for over 2000 years and are studied by divers today.

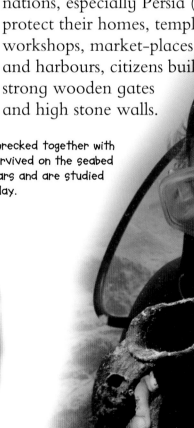

QUIZ

1. What was a city-state?
2. What was the centre of many cities?
3. What were coins made of?
4. How did the Greeks defend their cities?

Answers:
1. A city and the land around it
2. The agora (market-place) 3. Real silver 4. With strong wooden gates and high stone walls

Citizens, foreigners, slaves

▶ Slaves for sale. Men, women and children captured in war or snatched by pirates were put on display for rich families to buy.

224 Within most city-states, there were different classes of people. Citizens were men who had been born in the city-state, together with their wives and children. Foreigners were traders, sailors or travelling artists and scholars. Slaves belonged to their owners.

225 In wealthy city-states almost half the population were slaves. Household slaves did the shopping, cooking, housework and child care. Gangs of slave-labourers worked for rich citizens or city governments as builders, road-menders, miners and security guards. Slaves could be very badly treated. The conditions for slaves working in mines and on building sites were grim and many died.

1. What is democracy?
2. Where was it established?
3. What is an ostrakon?
4. What was it used for?

Answers:
1. Rule by the people 2. Athens 3. A piece of broken pottery 4. Voting to ban an unpopular person from Athens. Citizens scratched the person's name on the ostrakon

226
In 508 BC, Athenian leader Cleisthenes established a new system of government called 'democracy' (rule by the people). All male citizens over 18 years old could speak and vote at city Assemblies, elect the officials that ran their city-state and be elected as city councillors. Women, foreigners, children and slaves had no democratic rights.

227
In Athens, citizens could make speeches at the Assembly to propose new laws for their community. They served as jurors in the city-state law courts, hearing the evidence against accused criminals and deciding whether they were innocent or guilty. Citizens could also take part in debates on important government decisions, such as whether to declare war.

▼ You can see the names of two unpopular Athenian citizens scratched on these pieces of pottery. Left, top line: Themistokles. Right, top line: Kimon.

▼ Speeches at the Athenian Assembly were carefully timed (and kept short) so that all citizens would have a chance to share in the debate.

228
Once a year, Athenian citizens voted to ban unpopular people from their city for ten years. They scratched the name of the person they wanted to remove on an ostrakon (piece of broken pottery). If 6000 citizens (about a quarter of the whole Assembly) voted to ban the same man, he had to leave the city within ten days.

Mighty Athens

229 **Athens was the greatest city in Greece.** Between 510–431 BC, it was the leading Greek city-state. Athens owned some of the best farmland, a port with a fine harbour, fabulous silver mines and a well-trained citizen army. All these made it rich, strong and confident.

▶ A steep winding road leads up to the Parthenon temple from the city far below. On festival days, processions of citizens lead prize animals along it to sacrifice to the goddess Athena.

230 **The Acropolis ('high city') was a holy hill and ancient fortress that overlooked Athens.** Many fine buildings stood there, including the magnificent Parthenon temple. Built between 447 BC and 432 BC, it housed a 15-metre-high gold-and-marble statue of Athena, the city's guardian goddess.

231 In 490 and 480 BC, armies from Persia (now Iran) invaded Greece. They were defeated, but Greek city-states felt threatened. They joined together in a League against the Persians. Athens took charge of the League, built a splendid navy and sent soldiers and government officials to 'advise' other city-states. By 454 BC, Athens had taken control of most of Greece.

232 Athenian city leaders paid for fine works of art. They invited the best artists, architects, sculptors, scientists and scholars to live and work in their city, and gave money to build temples, monuments and public buildings. They vowed to make the city of Athens 'an education to Greece'.

233 Athenians are famous today – after more than 2000 years! Pericles was a great general and political leader. Socrates and Plato were philosophers and teachers who taught how to think and question. Aristotle was a scientist who pioneered a new way of studying by carefully observing and recording evidence.

Sparta

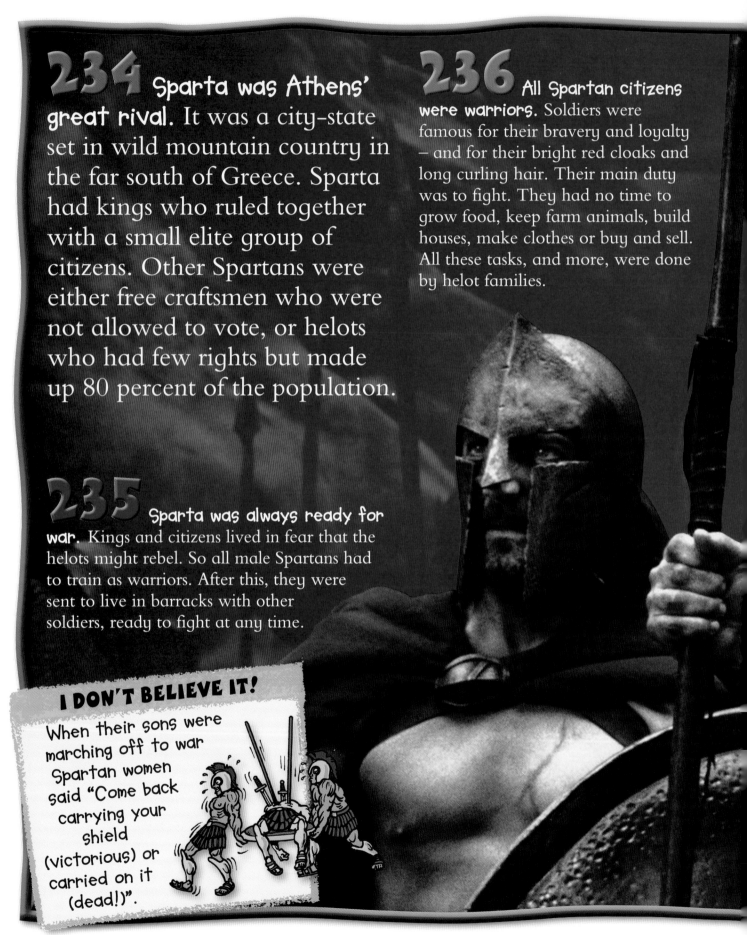

234 Sparta was Athens' great rival. It was a city-state set in wild mountain country in the far south of Greece. Sparta had kings who ruled together with a small elite group of citizens. Other Spartans were either free craftsmen who were not allowed to vote, or helots who had few rights but made up 80 percent of the population.

235 Sparta was always ready for war. Kings and citizens lived in fear that the helots might rebel. So all male Spartans had to train as warriors. After this, they were sent to live in barracks with other soldiers, ready to fight at any time.

236 All Spartan citizens were warriors. Soldiers were famous for their bravery and loyalty – and for their bright red cloaks and long curling hair. Their main duty was to fight. They had no time to grow food, keep farm animals, build houses, make clothes or buy and sell. All these tasks, and more, were done by helot families.

I DON'T BELIEVE IT!

When their sons were marching off to war Spartan women said "Come back carrying your shield (victorious) or carried on it (dead!)".

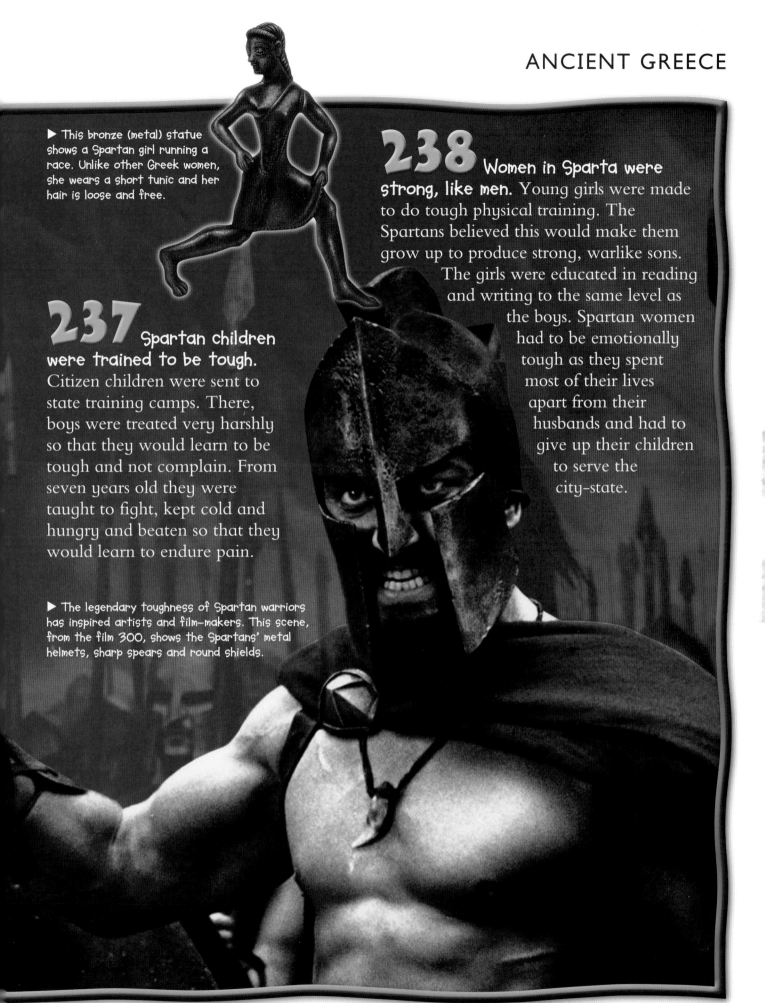

► This bronze (metal) statue shows a Spartan girl running a race. Unlike other Greek women, she wears a short tunic and her hair is loose and free.

238 Women in Sparta were strong, like men.

Young girls were made to do tough physical training. The Spartans believed this would make them grow up to produce strong, warlike sons. The girls were educated in reading and writing to the same level as the boys. Spartan women had to be emotionally tough as they spent most of their lives apart from their husbands and had to give up their children to serve the city-state.

237 Spartan children were trained to be tough.

Citizen children were sent to state training camps. There, boys were treated very harshly so that they would learn to be tough and not complain. From seven years old they were taught to fight, kept cold and hungry and beaten so that they would learn to endure pain.

► The legendary toughness of Spartan warriors has inspired artists and film-makers. This scene, from the film 300, shows the Spartans' metal helmets, sharp spears and round shields.

War on land and sea

239 As teenagers, all Greek male citizens were trained to fight. They had to be ready to defend their city whenever danger threatened. City-states also employed men as bodyguards and mercenary troops with special skills.

▼▶ Soldiers had different duties. Cavalrymen were messengers and spies. Peltasts had to move fast and were armed with javelins. Mercenaries fought for anyone who would pay them.

Peltast

Hoplite

Cavalry

Mercenary

240 Each soldier paid for his own weapons and armour. Most soldiers were hoplites (soldiers who fought on foot). Their most important weapons were swords and spears. Poor men could not afford swords or armour. Their only weapons were slings for shooting stones and simple wooden spears.

241 Soldiers rarely fought on horseback. At the start of a battle, hoplites lined up side by side with their shields overlapping, like a wall. Then they marched towards the enemy while the peltasts threw their javelins. When they were close enough, the hoplites used their spears to fight the enemy.

◀ A Corinthian-style helmet. Soldiers tried to protect themselves from injury with bronze helmets, breastplates, greaves (shin guards) and round wooden shields.

Ancient Greek soldiers rarely rode horses — because stirrups had not yet been invented. Without stirrups to support him, a soldier on horseback who hurled a spear or stabbed with a sword was likely to fall off backwards!

▼ Greek ships were made of wood. If they were holed below the waterline they sank very quickly.

242 City-states paid for fleets of fast, fearsome wooden warships, called triremes. Each ship had a crew of about 170 oarsmen who sat in three sets of seats, one above the other. They rowed the ship as fast as they could towards enemy vessels, hoping that the sharp, pointed ram at its prow would smash or sink them. The most famous naval battle in Greece was fought at Salamis, near Athens, in 480 BC, when the Greeks defeated the Persians.

Farming and fishing

243 **Cities were surrounded by fields and farms.** Everyone living inside the walls relied on country people to grow crops, raise animals and bring food to sell at city markets. Some rich families owned country farms as well as city houses and workshops. They paid for servants or slaves to work the land for them.

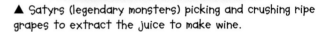

▲ Satyrs (legendary monsters) picking and crushing ripe grapes to extract the juice to make wine.

244 **Farmers worked hard to make a living.** The climate was harsh and they had no big machines to help them. Men ploughed the soil, cut down trees, sheared sheep and harvested grain. Women milked sheep and goats, made cheese, grew vegetables, kept chickens and bees and gathered wild herbs and berries. Children scared birds from crops and watched over sheep and goats.

▼ Sheep's wool was cleaned, combed, spun into thread then woven to make warm clothes, rugs and blankets.

245 **Grain, grapes and olives were the most valuable crops.** Barley was the chief grain crop. It was used to make porridge or flour. Grapes were dried in the sun, or trampled by bare feet to extract the juice. This was turned into wine. Olives were crushed to produce oil. This was used in cooking, for burning in lamps or for cleaning the skin.

246 The Greeks hunted in wild countryside.

Mountains and steep valleys were covered in thick forests. Wild creatures lived there, such as wolves, bears, boar and deer. Huntsmen tracked and killed them for their skins or meat. They also trapped wild birds and stole eggs from their nests, and caught small creatures to eat such as hares and rabbits.

▲ A wild boar hunt (top) pictured on a Greek pot made around 600 BC.

247 Seaside communities made a living from fishing.

Every day fishermen sailed out to catch tuna, mullet, squid, octopus and many other sea creatures. Villagers worked as boat-builders and sail-makers, or made ropes and fishing nets. Women prepared bait and preserved fish by drying or smoking to eat in winter.

▶ This wall painting from Minoan Crete shows a fisherman carrying home his catch of gleaming fresh fish.

248 Divers searched for sea produce to sell.

They plunged deep underwater, holding their breath for as long as they could. They searched for shellfish (to eat and use as dye for cloth) and sponges, which the Greeks used when bathing. Sponges also helped doctors soak up blood.

▼ A modern display of Greek seafood. Fish and shellfish might have been even better in ancient Greek times because the Mediterranean Sea was less polluted.

Food and drink

249
Greek food was plain, hearty and healthy. It included whole grains, cheese, beans and lentils, fruits, vegetables, olives and for special occasions – a little meat or fish.

▶ Preparing a meal in an open-air kitchen in the courtyard of a house. Food was cooked over a wood fire in a stone hearth.

250
Main meals were breakfast and dinner. Breakfast was bread dipped in olive oil or stale wine. Dinner was olives, then eggs, dried bean stew or hot barley porridge. This was followed by vegetables, fruit and honeycomb. Some people ate a light lunch of bread with fruit or cheese.

▼ A pottery bowl decorated with tasty-looking fish.

251
Greek cooking was very simple. Boiling, stewing or grilling were the only methods of cooking. Many foods were eaten raw, such as fruit, herbs and some shellfish. The Greeks disapproved of cooked dishes with lots of different ingredients, saying that they were too indulgent.

Mixing barley and honey to make cakes

Oil and wine stored in jars

Slabs of stone or pottery tiles for floor

All the cooking was done by hand

Stone hearth with metal racks for cooking

I DON'T BELIEVE IT!

A Greek dinner party might go on for hours and hours. Guests discussed sport and politics, listened to music, played silly games — and sometimes fell asleep between courses!

Cooking pots stored on wooden shelf

Walls of rough plaster

Table of scrubbed wood

252 **The Greeks enjoyed wine — but always mixed it with water.** Wine could be rough, strong and unsuitable for drinking. People also thought that drunkenness was shameful, except at parties for men only. They did not want to see their guests disgracing themselves.

253 **There might be hungry months in winter.** Meals were based on preserved foods and grain from the summer harvest. If these ran out, families went hungry. The only food preservation techniques were smoking, pickling, steeping in olive oil or drying in the sun.

254 **Dinner parties were for men only.** When husbands invited their male friends to a symposion (dinner party), their wives and daughters stayed away. At a party, male diners reclined on couches as slaves served food and wine.

▶ Male guests at a symposion relax while listening to a girl — probably a slave — playing the double flute.

Family life

255 **Families were very important.** A person's wealth, rank and occupation all depended on their family circumstances, as did the part they played in community life. Some families were very active in politics and had powerful friends – and enemies.

256 **Fathers were the heads of families.** They had power over everyone in their households – wives, children and slaves. However, families also worked as a team to find food, make a safe, comfortable home and train their children in all the skills they would need in adult life.

Bedrooms were upstairs

Pottery tiles

Mud-brick walls covered with plaster

Slaves cooked in the kitchen

Prayers were said around the altar each morning

257 **All Greek parents longed for a son.** Boys passed on the family name to the next generation and they could protect family property and run businesses or farms. However, girls had to be fed and housed at the family's expense, then they left to get married.

▲ Greek houses were designed to provide security and privacy. They had high, windowless outer walls and a hidden inner courtyard, which only the inhabitants and trusted visitors could see.

258 **Most girls married very young, aged around 13 years.** Their husbands, who were several years older, were chosen by their fathers for political or business reasons. A marriage linked two families together. Romantic love was not important in marriage – the Greeks thought it was dangerous!

▼ Weddings took place at dusk. The bride was driven to the bridegroom's family home, accompanied by guests carrying flaming wooden torches.

259 **Women did not have the same rights as men.** Many had strong opinions about city and community life. A few were also well-educated and interested in the latest ideas. However, according to the law, women could not vote, make a public speech or take any part in politics.

260 **Funerals were important family occasions.** Wives and daughters spent most of their lives at home but they were allowed to attend family funerals. All family members said prayers and made offerings to the gods in memory of the dead person.

Education

QUIZ

1. At what age did boys start school?
2. Name three subjects boys studied there.
3. Name two favourite Greek sports.

Answers:
1. Around seven years old
2. Reading, writing, arithmetic, how to sing or play a musical instrument, how to debate and recite poetry 3. Running, jumping, wrestling, throwing the javelin

261 From their earliest days, children were expected to play their part in the family. This meant being well-behaved, obedient, sharing family worship of the gods and showing respect to parents.

▲ A schoolroom scene, pictured on a Greek pot, showing a music lesson, a writing lesson and a slave. The slave is there to make sure that his master's son behaves and works hard.

262 From around seven years old, boys from wealthy families went to school. They learnt reading, writing, simple arithmetic, how to sing or play a musical instrument and how to debate and recite poetry. They also practised Greek sports such as running, jumping, wrestling and throwing the javelin.

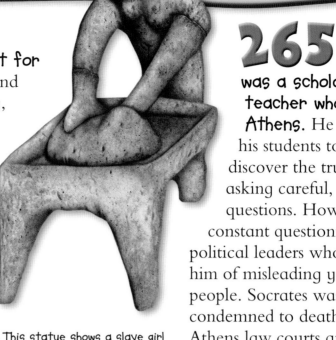

263
School was not for girls. They stayed at home and learned skills such as spinning, weaving and cookery. Wealthy women taught their daughters how to read and write, keep accounts, manage a big household and give orders. Older women also passed on traditional songs and dances so that girls could take part in religious festivals.

▲ This statue shows a slave girl mixing flour, yeast and water to make bread.

265
Socrates was a scholar and teacher who lived in Athens. He encouraged his students to try to discover the truth by asking careful, thoughtful questions. However, his constant questioning alarmed political leaders who accused him of misleading young people. Socrates was condemned to death by the Athens law courts and given poison. He died in 399 BC.

264
Most boys left school when they were 14 years old. Older boys might study with local scholars or sophists (travelling teachers). Around 380 BC, a man called Plato opened a study centre in Athens called the Academy. He planned to train young men to work for the city-state, but attracted the best students in Greece who became famous for their brilliant ideas.

▶ Plato believed that thinking and learning were essential for a good life.

Clothes and fashion

266 Greek clothes were just draped around the body. They were loose and flowing, for comfort in the hot summer months. For extra warmth in winter, both men and women draped a thick woolly himation (cloak) over their shoulders.

267 Each piece of cloth used to make a garment was specially made. It had to be the right length and width to fit the wearer. All cloth was handwoven, usually by women in their homes. Cool, smooth linen was the favourite cloth for summer. In winter, Greeks preferred cosy wool. Very rich people wore fine clothes of silk imported from India.

▶ Men's clothing was designed for action. Young men wore short tunics so they could work – and fight – easily. Older men's robes were longer.

◀ Women's clothing was modest and draped the body from top to toe. Respectable women covered their heads and faces with a veil when they went outside the house.

MAKE A GREEK CHITON

You will need:
Length of cloth twice as wide as your outstretched arms and half your height
safety pins   belt or length of cord

1. Fold the cloth in half.

2. Fasten two edges of the cloth together with safety pins, leaving a gap of about 30 cm in the middle.

3. Pull the cloth over your head so that the safety pins sit on your shoulders.

4. Fasten the belt or cord around your waist. Pull some of the cloth over the belt so that the cloth is level with your knees.

268 Women – and men – took care of their skin. To keep their skin smooth and supple, men and women rubbed themselves all over with olive oil. Rich women also used sunshades or face powder to achieve a fashionably pale complexion. They did not want to look sun-tanned – that was for farm workers, slaves – and men!

Before 500 BC

500–300 BC

After 300 BC

▲ Before 500 BC, long, natural hairstyles were popular. Between 500–300 BC, women tied their hair up and held it in place with ribbons or scarves. After 300 BC, curled styles and jewelled hair ornaments were popular and men shaved off their beards.

269 Curls were very fashionable. Women grew their hair long and tied it up with ribbons or headbands, leaving long curls trailing over their shoulders. Men, except for Spartan warriors, had short curly hair. Male and female slaves had their hair cropped very short – this was a shameful sign.

270 The Greeks liked to look good and admired fit, slim, healthy bodies. Women were praised for their grace and beauty. Men were admired for their strong figures, and often went without clothes when training for war or taking part in sports competitions. Top athletes became celebrities, and were asked by artists to pose for them as models.

◄ Athletes and their trainer (left) pictured on a Greek vase.

271 Sponges, showers and swimming helped the Greeks keep clean. Most houses did not have piped water. So people washed themselves by standing under waterfalls, swimming in streams or squeezing a big sponge full of water over their heads, like a shower.

Gods and goddesses

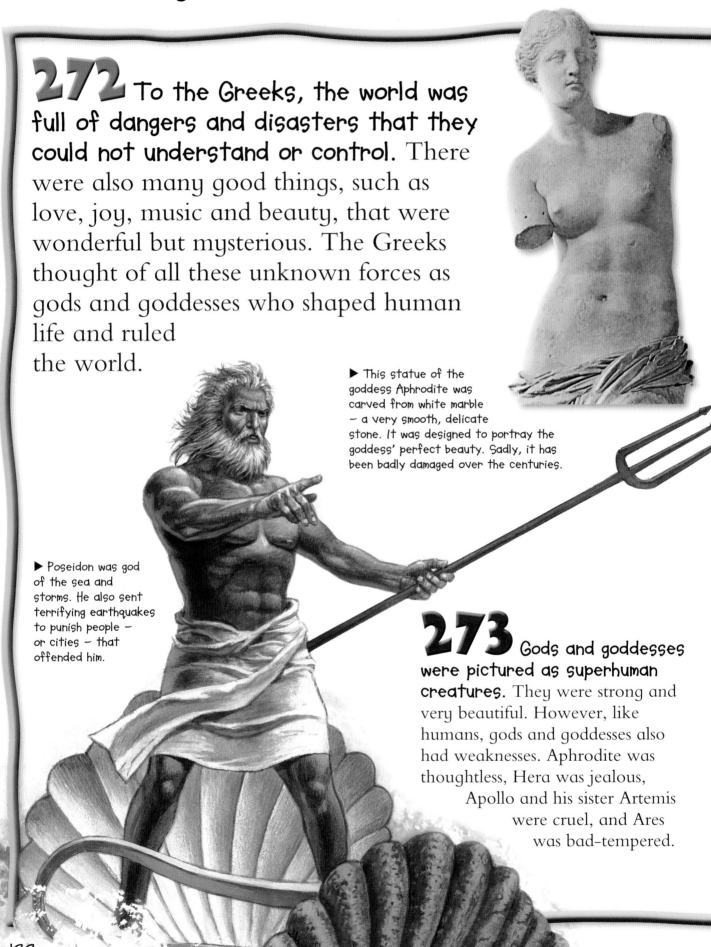

272 To the Greeks, the world was full of dangers and disasters that they could not understand or control. There were also many good things, such as love, joy, music and beauty, that were wonderful but mysterious. The Greeks thought of all these unknown forces as gods and goddesses who shaped human life and ruled the world.

▶ This statue of the goddess Aphrodite was carved from white marble – a very smooth, delicate stone. It was designed to portray the goddess' perfect beauty. Sadly, it has been badly damaged over the centuries.

▶ Poseidon was god of the sea and storms. He also sent terrifying earthquakes to punish people – or cities – that offended him.

273 Gods and goddesses were pictured as superhuman creatures. They were strong and very beautiful. However, like humans, gods and goddesses also had weaknesses. Aphrodite was thoughtless, Hera was jealous, Apollo and his sister Artemis were cruel, and Ares was bad-tempered.

▲ Odysseus and his shipmates were surrounded by the Sirens – beautiful half-women, half-bird monsters. They sang sweet songs, calling sailors towards dangerous rocks where their ships were wrecked.

274 The Greeks believed in magic spirits and monsters. These included Gorgons who turned men to stone, and Sirens – bird-women whose song lured sailors to their doom. They also believed in witchcraft and curses and tried to fight against them. People painted magic eyes on the prows of their ships to keep a look-out for evil.

275 Individuals were often anxious to see what the future would bring. They believed that oracles (holy messengers) could see the future. The most famous oracles were at Delphi, where a drugged priestess answered questions, and at Dodona, where the leaves of sacred trees whispered words from the gods.

► Herakles was a hero – a man who became a god. He performed amazing feats of strength and fought against many monsters. This statue shows him killing a centaur, half-man, half-horse.

276 Poets and dramatists retold myths and legends about the gods. Some stories were explanations of natural events – thunder was the god Zeus shaking his fist in anger. Others explored bad thoughts and feelings shared by gods and humans, such as greed and disloyalty.

Temples and festivals

277 In Greece and the lands where the Greeks settled, we can still see remains of huge, beautiful temples. They were built as holy homes for gods and goddesses. Each city-state had its own guardian god and many temples housed a huge, lifelike statue of him or her. People hoped that the god's spirit might visit them and live in the statue for a while.

▶ This gigantic statue of the goddess Athena was 15 metres high and was made of gold and ivory. It stood inside her finest temple, the Parthenon in Athens. In her right hand, Athena holds Nike, the goddess of victory.

278
As well as visiting a temple, people hoped – or feared – that they might meet a god or goddess in a forest or on a mountain top. It was thought that all the gods met at Mount Olympus to feast, love, quarrel and make plans. Another high peak, Mount Parnassus, was sacred to the Muses – nine graceful goddesses who guided the arts, such as music and drama.

▲ The summit of the tallest mountain in Greece, Mount Olympus (1951 metres), was often hidden in clouds. It was remote, dangerous and mysterious – a suitable home for the mighty gods.

▼ The first temples were made of wood and shaped like ordinary houses. By around AD 600, temples were built of stone.

279
People offered prayers and sacrifices (gifts) to their gods and goddesses. Gifts might be just a few drops of wine or a valuable live animal. The meat of the sacrifice was cooked and shared among the worshippers and the bones and skin were burned on the altar. People thought that smoke carried their prayers up to the gods.

c. 800 BC tree trunks hold up the roof. Small inner room.

c. 600 BC tree trunks replaced by stone columns. More rooms inside.

280
City-states held festivals to honour their guardian gods. There would be a procession towards the city's main temple or to a shrine (holy place). At temples, crowds watched priests and priestesses making special sacrifices. At shrines, citizens might take part in secret rituals. Afterwards there could be music and drama or sports contests.

c. 440 BC temples are huge, with rows of columns and carved decorations.

Olympic Games

281 **The Olympic Games began as a festival to honour Zeus.** Over the centuries, it grew into the greatest sports event in the Greek world. A huge festival complex was built at Olympia with a temple, sports tracks, seats for 40,000 spectators, a campsite and rooms for visitors and a field full of stalls selling food and drink.

▶ Victory! The Greeks believed that winners were chosen by the gods. The first known Olympic Games was held in 776 BC, though the festival may have begun years earlier.

282 **Every four years athletes travelled from all over Greece to take part in the Olympic Games.** They had to obey strict rules – respect for Zeus, no fights among competitors and no weapons anywhere near the sports tracks. In return they claimed protection – the holy Olympic Peace. Anyone who attacked them on their journeys was severely punished.

QUIZ

1. When was the first Olympic Games held?
2. Could women go to the Olympic Games?
3. What did winning athletes wear on their heads?

Answers:
1. 776 BC, though the festival may have begun years earlier. 2. No. There was a separate women's games held 3. Crowns of holy laurel leaves

126

▲ Boxers did not wear gloves. Instead they wrapped their hands in bandages.

283 The most popular events were running, long jump, wrestling and boxing. Spectators might also watch chariot races, athletes throwing the discus and javelin or weightlifting contests. The most prestigious event was the 200-metre sprint. There was also a dangerous fighting contest called *pankration* (total power).

284 Many events featured weapons or skills that were needed in war. One of the most gruelling competitions was a race wearing heavy battle armour. The main Olympic Games were for men only – women could not take part. There was a separate women's games held at Olympia on different years from the men's competitions.

▲ Throwing the discus was a test of strength and balance. It was also useful training for war.

▲ Swimmer Michael Phelps sets a new world record at the Beijing Olympics, 2008. The modern Olympics is modelled on the ancient games and since 1896 has remained the world's greatest sports festival.

285 Athletes who won Olympic contests were honoured as heroes. They were crowned with wreaths of holy laurel leaves and given valuable prizes of olive oil, fine clothes and pottery. Poets composed songs in their praise and their home city-states often rewarded them with free food and lodgings for life!

▶ A crown of laurel leaves was given to winning athletes as a sign of their god-like strength and speed.

Plays and poems

286 **Greek drama originated at religious festivals.** In the earliest rituals, priests and priestesses sometimes played the part of gods or goddesses. They acted out stories told about them or local heroes. Over the years, these ancient rituals changed into a new art form – drama.

I DON'T BELIEVE IT!

Music for poetry was played on a lyre. This was rather like a small harp, but had a real (dead) hollow tortoise shell as a sounding-box!

287 **Drama became so popular that many city-states built splendid new open-air theatres.** Greek theatres were built in a half-circle shape with tiers (raised rows) of seats looking down over an open space for performers. Most seats were filled by men – women were banned from many plays.

▶ The theatre at Epidaurus, in southern Greece, is one of the largest built by the ancient Greeks. It had seats for over 10,000 spectators.

288
All the parts in a play were performed by men. They wore masks, wigs and elaborate costumes to look like women or magic spirits and monsters. Some theatres had ladders and cranes so that actors playing gods could appear to fly or sit among the clouds.

289
In some city-states, especially Athens, drama remained an important part of several religious festivals. Writers competed for prizes for the best plays. They wrote serious plays called tragedies and lively comedies. Some lasted all day long. Others had extra 'satyr plays' added on. These were short, funny pieces.

▶ Actors wore masks to show which character they were playing. Bright-coloured masks were for cheerful characters and dark-coloured masks were more gloomy. Some masks were double-sided so that the actors could change parts quickly.

290
Plays were written like poetry. The main actors were always accompanied by singers and dancers. Poems were also recited to music. Tunes were sad for tragic poems or rousing for those about war. Poets performed at men's dinner parties and in rich families' homes. Public storytellers entertained crowds by singing poems in the streets.

Barbarian – or monster – with wild, shaggy hair

Angry young man

Huge, funnel-shaped mouths helped the actors' words reach the audience

Masks with beards and bald heads were for actors playing old men

Scientists and thinkers

291 The Greeks liked to ask questions and discuss things. Although they believed in gods and magic, they also wanted to investigate the world in a practical way. Some mathematics and astronomy was learned from the Egyptians and Babylonians. Then the Greeks used this knowledge to find out more for themselves.

▶ Hipparchus (170–126 BC) observed and recorded the position of over 800 stars and worked out a way of measuring their brightness.

292 Mathematicians and astronomers made important discoveries. Aristarchus was the first to understand that the Earth travels around the Sun. Hipparchus mapped the stars. Thales discovered mathematical laws about circles and triangles. Pythagoras worked out the mathematics behind music and measured the movements of the Sun and the Moon.

293
Many people believed that illness was a punishment sent by the gods. However doctors, led by Hippocrates (460–370 BC), tried to cure people with good food, fresh air, exercise and herbal medicines. They carefully observed patients for signs of illness and recorded the results of their prescriptions. That way they could prove scientifically which treatments worked best for each disease.

▼ Archimedes was the most famous Greek engineer. He invented (or improved) a spiral pump to make water flow uphill, for example, from rivers into fields.

▲ This stone carving shows a doctor treating an injured arm. Greek doctors were some of the first in the world to treat patients scientifically.

Handle turns wooden screw

Water is lifted round and round and then pushed out

Water is pulled in as the screw turns

294
Engineers designed many clever machines. Speakers at the Athenian Assembly were timed by a water-powered clock and there were machines that used hot air to open temple doors. Archimedes (287–211 BC) discovered how objects float and how they balance. He also designed a 'sun gun' (huge glass lens) to focus the Sun's rays on enemy ships to set them on fire.

295
Greek thinkers thought about thinking! As well as investigating the world and creating new inventions they wanted to understand society. They asked questions such as 'How do we think?', 'How do we see and feel?', 'What is good?' and 'How can we live the best lives?'.

Ancient Greek heritage

296 The ancient Greeks lived over 2000 years ago, but still influence our lives today. Many people still admire the democratic system of government that Greek city-states invented. The Olympic Games, revived in 1896, is the greatest sporting contest in the world. And today's plays, films, musicals and TV series have their origins in Greek religious drama.

▼ A Greek temple on Sicily. Its massive ruins still impress visitors today.

297 Many modern words and names have developed from ancient Greek originals. Greek-inspired words include 'telephone', 'television' and 'music'. Greek personal names, such as Chloe, Penelope, Jason and Philip, are still popular today. Many places around the Mediterranean have names that reveal their Greek origins – Naples, in Italy, was Neapolis (New City) to the Greeks.

298 Today's ways of writing are copied from the ancient Greeks. The Greek alphabet was invented around 1000–800 BC, after scribes in Phoenicia (now Lebanon) became the first to use written signs (letters) to represent separate sounds. The Greeks made good use of that amazing idea and passed their alphabet on to the Romans. From there, it spread throughout Europe – and then all round the world.

▲ In Washington DC, the White House (home of the President of the USA) has design features borrowed from Greek buildings, such as the porch with tall columns.

300 Traces of ancient Greek civilization still survive. When Greece was conquered by invaders, many important writings and works of art were lost and buildings were destroyed. Some survived because they were copied by the Romans. Greek culture was rediscovered by European thinkers around AD 1400–1600 and inspired artists for centuries. Today, the ruins of great Greek buildings still survive. Poems and plays are still read and acted and many works of art are preserved in museums.

299 We copy Greek designs for clothes and buildings. Fashion designers dress models and filmstars in styles copied from Greek clothes. For hundreds of years, impressive buildings have included Greek design features, such as tall, fluted (ridged) columns. Even very modern buildings make use of Greek ideas about shape and size.

▼ Repairing the Parthenon, Athens, 2004. Ancient Greek buildings are national treasures that make citizens and governments feel proud.

133

ANCIENT ROME

River Tiber
This was a source of water for the people of Rome

Circus Maximus
A huge stadium built to stage public entertainment

Imperial Palace
First built around AD 30 the palace remained in use for 300 years

Temple of the Divine Claudius
A temple dedicated to the patron gods of the imperial family

301 The Italian city of Rome was once the hub of one of the world's greatest empires. An empire is made up of lots of countries governed by one ruler. Around 1000 BC Rome was a village on the River Tiber, but it soon grew rich and powerful. It was busy and exciting, with many beautiful buildings. By 200 BC the Romans ruled most of Italy, and started to invade neighbouring lands.

Forum
The political and business centre of the empire

Temple of Apollo
The Greek god Apollo became popular in Rome in later years

Colosseum
Famous amphitheatre where gladiatorial fights were staged

Baths of Trajan
Built by the Emperor Trajan as a place of relaxation for citizens

Ludus Magnus
Training school and barracks for gladiators who fought in the Colosseum

Servian Wall
The stone wall around Rome built around 490 BC. It was replaced by the larger Aurelian Wall in about AD 275 and was allowed to fall into ruin

Aqua Claudia
Aqueduct that brought fresh water to Rome from springs 72 kilometres to the southeast

▲ The Forum was the central hub of Rome. It was the home of government and a busy marketplace. The rest of the city contained places for leisure, sport and religion, and was filled with houses and blocks of flats where the citizens lived.

Capital city

302 **Over one million people lived in Rome.** By around AD 300, Rome was the largest city in the world. There were citizens who could vote and serve in the army, and there were non-citizens who did not have these rights. The government was run by wealthy nobles and knights. Plebeians (ordinary people) were usually fairly poor but were citizens of Rome. Slaves were non-citizens. They were not free to leave their owners and had no rights.

▼ In 44 BC the dictator Julius Caesar built the Curia Julia as a meeting house for the Senate of Rome. The building later became a church and has survived intact to the present day.

303 **The Forum was the centre of Rome.** It was originally an open space at the foot of the Capitoline Hill, and was used as a market place, meeting place and picnic area. Later, government buildings were erected here, including offices for the Senate, law courts and temples.

River Tiber

Aurelian Wall

Servian Wall

304 Rome was very well protected. It was surrounded by 50 kilometres of strong stone walls to keep out attackers. Visitors had to enter the city through one of its 37 gates, which were guarded by soldiers and watchmen.

◀ In AD 275 the old Servian Wall of about 380 BC was replaced by the Aurelian Wall that protected the new, larger city of Rome. The new wall was 19 kilometres long, 16 metres tall and had 383 towers. It remained in use until the siege of 1870.

306 Rome relied on its drains. The city was so crowded that without good drains the citizens could have caught diseases from sewage and died. The largest sewer, called the *cloaca maxima*, was so high and wide that a horse and cart could drive through it.

305 The Romans were great water engineers. They designed aqueducts (raised channels to carry water from streams in distant hills and mountains to the city). The homes of rich citizens were supplied with running water carried in lead pipes. Ordinary people had to drink from public fountains.

I DON'T BELIEVE IT!

Roman engineers also designed public lavatories. They were convenient but not at all private — users had to sit on rows of seats, side by side!

▶ The Romans built the Pont Du Gard in the south of France — a 360-metre-long aqueduct supported on three tiers of arches.

Home sweet home

▲ A reconstruction of a house belonging to a rich family in the city of Pompeii. This grand room, the Atrium, was where guests were entertained.

QUIZ

1. What were Roman blocks of flats known as?

2. What are pictures made with coloured stones or glass called?

3. How did Romans heat their homes?

Answers:
1. Insulae 2. Mosaics
3. Wealthy families had underfloor heating, ordinary families used fires

307 **Rich Romans had more than one home.** Rome was noisy, dirty and smelly. Wealthy citizens would often have a house just outside the city (a *villa urbana*), or a big house with land in the country (a *villa rustica*) in which they spent the summer months.

308
The Romans built the world's first high-rise apartments. Most of the people who lived in Ostia, a busy port close to Rome, had jobs connected with trade, such as shipbuilders and money-changers. They lived in blocks of flats known as *insulae*. A typical block was three or four storeys high, with up to 100 small, dirty, crowded rooms.

▼ On the ground floor of an *insula* were shops, and on the first floor were flats and apartments for families. The poorest families lived in single rooms on the top floor.

310
Many homes had a pool, but it wasn't used for swimming! Decorative pools were built in the central courtyards of large homes, surrounded by plants and statues. Some had fountains. In others mosaics (pictures made of tiny coloured stones or squares of glass) covered the floor.

311
Rome's fire brigade was made up of specially trained freed slaves. People who could not afford central heating warmed their rooms with fires in clay pots, which often set houses alight.

309
Wealthy family homes had underfloor central heating. Blasts of hot air, warmed by a wood-burning furnace, circulated in channels built beneath the floor. Slaves chopped wood and stoked the fire.

▶ Some public buildings and wealthy homes had a heating system called a hypocaust. Hot air from a fire tended by a slave passed through spaces under the floor and up the walls to keep the rooms warm.

Space in walls for hot air to circulate

Fire in basement

Space under floor for hot air to circulate

Buying and selling

312 Roman ships travelled the known world. Merchants sailed around the Empire and beyond looking for trade. Ships reached as far as India to the east and Iceland to the north. Luxury goods, such as silk, spices and furs, were the most sought after.

QUIZ

1. How many levels was Trajan's Market built on?

2. Who wore jewellery in ancient Rome – men or women?

3. Did Roman ships sail to Iceland?

Answers:
1. Five 2. Both men and women wore jewellery 3. Yes – they sailed there to trade

▼ A Roman ship approaches Dubris (now Dover) in Britain in AD 90 as a lighthouse is built on the cliff to help guide ships into harbour.

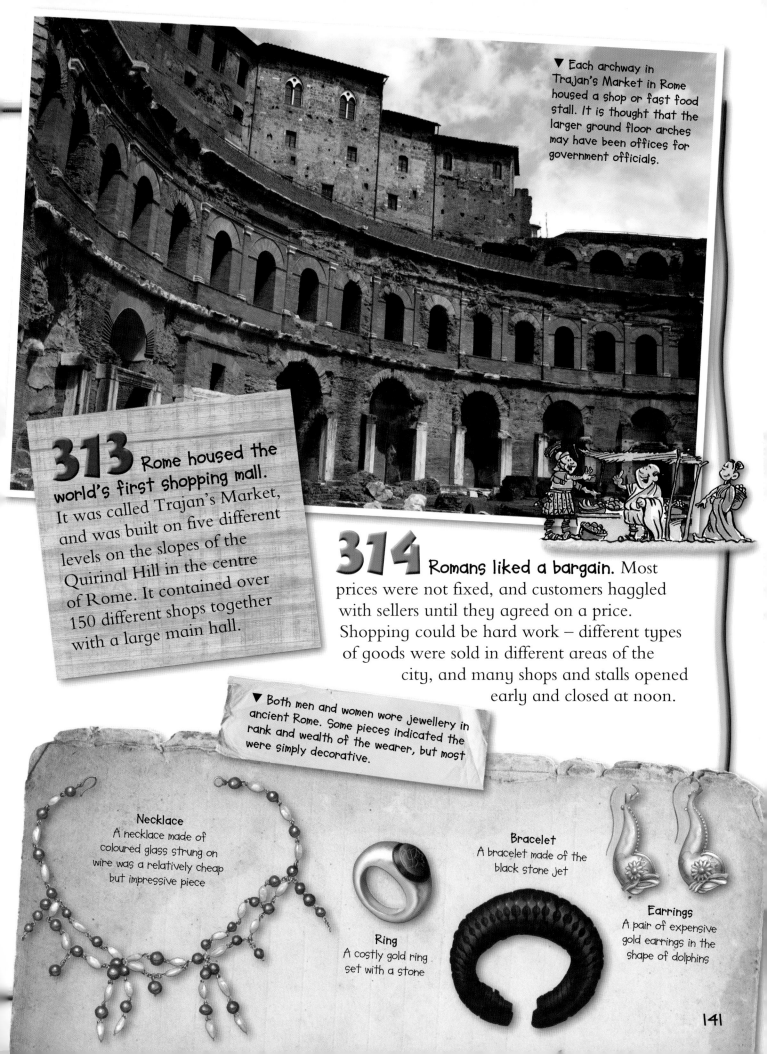

▼ Each archway in Trajan's Market in Rome housed a shop or fast food stall. It is thought that the larger ground floor arches may have been offices for government officials.

313 Rome housed the world's first shopping mall. It was called Trajan's Market, and was built on five different levels on the slopes of the Quirinal Hill in the centre of Rome. It contained over 150 different shops together with a large main hall.

314 Romans liked a bargain. Most prices were not fixed, and customers haggled with sellers until they agreed on a price. Shopping could be hard work – different types of goods were sold in different areas of the city, and many shops and stalls opened early and closed at noon.

▼ Both men and women wore jewellery in ancient Rome. Some pieces indicated the rank and wealth of the wearer, but most were simply decorative.

Necklace
A necklace made of coloured glass strung on wire was a relatively cheap but impressive piece

Ring
A costly gold ring set with a stone

Bracelet
A bracelet made of the black stone jet

Earrings
A pair of expensive gold earrings in the shape of dolphins

141

Eating and drinking

Figs   Grapes

▲ Romans ate large quantities of fruit raw, cooked or dried. Grapes were crushed and made into wine.

315 Most Romans ate little during the day. They had bread and water for breakfast and a snack of bread, cheese or fruit around midday. The main meal was eaten in the late afternoon, and in rich households it had three courses. Poor people ate simple food: soups made with lentils and onions, barley porridge, peas, cabbage and cheap cuts of meat stewed in vinegar.

ROMAN FOOD

Patina de piris (Pear soufflé)

Ingredients:

1 kg pears (peeled and cored)
6 eggs (beaten)   4 tbsp honey
oil   pinch of salt   ½ tsp cumin
ground pepper to taste

Ask an adult to help you with this recipe. Mash the pears together with the pepper, cumin, honey, and a bit of oil. Add the beaten eggs and put into a casserole dish. Cook for approximately 30 minutes in a moderate oven. Serve with a little pepper sprinkled on top.

► An engraved drinking cup made in Gaul, France, in about AD 380. The skills of making glass were lost after the fall of Rome.

316 Only rich people had their own kitchen. They could afford to employ a chef with slaves to help him. Ordinary people went to *popinae* (cheap eating houses) for their main meal, or bought ready-cooked snacks from roadside fast food stalls.

Oregano

Black pepper

Juniper berries

Coriander seeds

Thyme

Garlic

Olives

Asparagus

Celery

Lentils

Radishes

▲ Herbs and spices added flavour to dishes. Pepper and coriander came from across the Indian Ocean and were very expensive.

▲ Vegetables were eaten raw or cooked in stews. Garlic was a favourite ingredient used in many dishes.

317 **At parties, the Romans ate lying down.** Men and women lay on long couches arranged around a table. They also often wore crowns of flowers, and took off their sandals before entering the dining room.

Sardine

▼ A relief shows a rich woman reclining on a couch with her child while a slave or servant brings in a dish of food.

▲ Fish and meat were relatively expensive so poorer people rarely ate them. Sardines could be dried and salted for storage.

318 **Roman boys learnt to speak well.** At school they were taught reading, maths and public speaking – skills they would need in their careers. There were no newspapers or TVs, so politicians, army leaders and government officials had to make speeches to explain their plans and policies to Roman crowds.

▼ Boys attended school from seven years old. At 16, their education was complete.

319 **Roman girls did not go to school.** They stayed at home, where their mothers or women slaves taught them household tasks, such as how to cook, clean, weave cloth and look after children. Girls from wealthy families, or families who ran a business, also learned to read, write and keep accounts.

320 **Many of the best teachers were slaves.** Schoolmasters and private tutors often came from Greece. They were purchased by wealthy people who wanted to give their sons a good education. The Greeks had a long tradition of learning, which the Romans admired.

▼ An inscription in Latin placed over the doorway of a house. It means 'Peace to those coming in'.

PAX INTRANTIBVS
SALVS EXEVNTIBVS

Ink pot

Pens

R

Stylus, to use with a wax tablet

Wax tablet

321 **The Romans did not write on paper.** They used thin slices of wood for letters and day-to-day business. For notes Romans used flat, wooden boards covered with wax, as the wax could be smoothed over and used again. For important documents that they wanted to keep, they used cleaned, polished calfskin or papyrus.

322 **Romans made ink from soot.** Black ink was a mixture of soot, vinegar and a sticky gum that oozed from tree bark. Some Roman writing has survived for almost 2000 years.

▶ A list of Roman words and their English meanings. Some modern words are based on Roman words. For instance the word 'library' comes from *liber*.

ROMAN	ENGLISH
EPISTOLA	LETTER
VELLUM	CALFSKIN
GRAMMATICUS	SCHOOLMASTER
PAEDAGOGUS	PRIVATE TUTOR
STYLUS	WRITING STICK
BIBLIOTHECA	LIBRARY
LIBER	BOOK
LIBRARII	SLAVES WHO WORKED IN A LIBRARY

▲ Quick notes were scribbled on a wax tablet and wiped clean later. More important messages were written in ink onto vellum (calfskin parchment).

324 **Many Romans read standing up.** It took time to learn how to read from a papyrus scroll. Most were at least 10 metres long. Readers held the scroll in their right hand, a stick in their left, and unrolled a small section of the scroll at a time.

323 **Many boys did not go to school.** Poorer boys who needed to earn a living would get a job in a workshop or on a farm. They learned how to run a business or carry out a trade. At 16 they might set up in business on their own.

Family life

325 **A Roman father had the power of life and death over his family.** By law each family was led by a man – usually the oldest surviving male. He was known as the *paterfamilias* (father of a family). The house and its contents belonged to him. He had the right to punish any family members who misbehaved – even his mother and other older female relatives.

▶ A Roman wedding. The bridge and groom hold hands while their families watch. Most marriages were arranged by the families for business or political reasons. The couple being married had little say in the decision.

326 **Families included more than blood relations.** To the Romans, the word 'family' meant all the people living and working together in the same household. So families included many different slaves and servants, as well as a husband, wife and their children.

◀ The Romans gave a good luck charm, called a *bulla*, to their babies.

I DON'T BELIEVE IT!

The Romans invented Valentine's Day, but called it Lupercalia. Boys picked a girl's name from a hat, and she was meant to be their girlfriend for the year!

327 Life in Rome was easier if you were a boy. Boys were valued because they would carry on the family name, and might bring fame and honour to a family through their careers. For Roman girls, childhood was short. They were often married by the age of 12, and many had become mothers by the time they were 15.

328 Families liked to keep pets. Many statues and paintings show children playing with animals. Dogs, cats and doves were all popular. Some families also kept ornamental fish and tame deer.

▶ Roman women play with a fawn (young deer), while enjoying a day in the countryside.

329 Funerals were very elaborate. A funeral was a chance for a family to show off to their friends and neighbours. Huge feasts were provided, speeches were made and actors played out incidents from the life of the dead person.

◀ Some Romans cremated their dead. The ashes were then put in an urn before being buried, often in a family tomb.

147

Roman style

330 **Most Roman clothes were made without sewing.** Loose-fitting robes made of long strips of cloth were draped round the body and held in place by pins, brooches or belts. Most women wore layers – a *tunica* (thin shift), a *stola* (long, sleeveless dress), and a *palla* (cloak). Men wore a *colobium* (knee-length tunic) with a semi-circular cloak called a toga over the top.

▶ Three different ways that women could wear the *palla,* which was often made of costly fabric.

331 **Clothes were different depending on how important you were.** Ordinary men wore plain white togas, but government leaders, called senators, appeared in togas with a purple stripe around the edge. Rich men and women wore robes made of smooth, fine-quality wool and silk. Ordinary people's clothes were much rougher.

◀ This mosaic shows a man wearing a toga. The toga could be worn only by men who were citizens of Rome. Many men had a special toga of costly coloured linen to wear at special events.

▶ A gold fibula, or pin. These small pins were used to hold cloaks and tunics in place.

332 Clothes told the world who you were.
People from many different cultures lived in lands ruled by Rome, and they wore different styles of clothes. Men from Egypt wore wigs and linen kilts. Celtic women from northern Europe wore long, woollen shawls, woven in brightly coloured checks. Celtic men wore trousers.

◀ Sandals known as *crepidae* were worn by men and women all year round.

TOGA TIME!
1. Ask an adult for a blanket or sheet. White is best, like the Romans.
2. Drape the sheet over your left shoulder. Now pass the rest behind your back.
3. Pull the sheet across your front, so that you're wrapped up in it.
4. Finally, drape the last end over your right hand and there you have it, a Roman toga!

333 Boots were made for walking!
Soldiers and travellers wore lace-up boots with thick leather soles studded with iron nails. Other footwear included *socci*, loose-fitting slippers to wear indoors. Farmers wore shoes made of a single piece of ox-hide wrapped round the foot, called *carbatinae*. There were also *crepidae* – comfortable lace-up sandals with open toes.

▲ These Roman sandals have metal studs in the soles to make sure that they don't wear down too quickly.

Looking good

334 Roman hairstyles changed according to fashion. All free-born women grew their hair long, as short hair was a sign of slavery. In early Roman times plain and simple styles were fashionable. Later on, most women wore their hair tied back. Men usually wore their hair short, and were mostly clean shaven.

▲ Hairstyle fashions changed frequently. This lady's style dates to about AD 90.

335 The Romans painted their faces. They admired pale, smooth skin. Women, and some men, used stick-on patches of cloth called *splenia* to cover spots, and wore make-up. They used crushed chalk or white lead as face-powder, red ochre (crumbly earth) for blusher, plant juice for lipstick and wood-ash or powdered antimony (a silvery metal) as eye-liner.

◄ Most rich women had slaves whose job it was to keep their hair perfect.

336 Blonde hair was highly prized.

Most Romans had wiry, dark-brown hair, so delicate, blonde hair was admired by fashionable people because it was unusual. Women used vinegar and lye (an early form of soap, made from urine and wood-ash) to bleach their own hair.

337 Romans liked to smell sweet.

Olive oil was rubbed into the skin to cleanse and soften, then scraped off with a curved metal tool. Ingredients for perfume came from many different lands – flowers from southern Europe, spices from India and Africa, and sweet-smelling bark and resin from Arabia.

Roses to make perfume

Star anise to make perfume

Saffron for eyeshadow

Herbs such as majoram to make perfume

▲ Many plants were used to make perfume and cosmetics.

339 Tonsors (Roman barbers) did more than shave.

They worked in small shops, and passed on news and gossip about famous people, so some men went every day to catch up on the latest events. A boy's first shave – his *tonsora* – was a sign that he was an adult man.

338 Combs were made from bone, ivory or wood.

Like combs today, they were designed to smooth and untangle hair, and were sometimes worn as hair ornaments. But they had another, less pleasant, purpose – they were used for combing out all the little nits and lice!

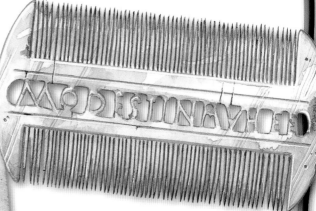

▲ Fine combs such as this teased out tangles and removed pests.

Bath time

▼ The Roman baths at Bath, in Somerset. Only the actual water bath is original, the other buildings date from the 18th century.

340 The Romans went to public baths to relax. These huge buildings were more than just places to get clean. They were also fitness centres and meeting places. Visitors could take part in sports, such as wrestling, do exercises, have a massage or a haircut. They could buy scented oils and perfumes, read books, eat snacks or admire works of art in the bath's own sculpture gallery!

341 Men and women could not bathe together. Women usually went to the baths in the mornings, while most men were at work. Men went to the baths in the afternoons.

I DON'T BELIEVE IT!

Although the Romans liked bathing, they visited the baths only once in every nine days. Basins of water were used in between baths to wash hands or faces.

342

Bathing wasn't simple – there were lots of stages. First bathers sat in a very hot room full of steam. Then they went into a hot, dry room, where a slave removed all the sweat and dirt from their skin, using a metal scraper and olive oil. To cool off, they went for a swim in a tepid pool. Finally, they jumped into a bracing cold pool.

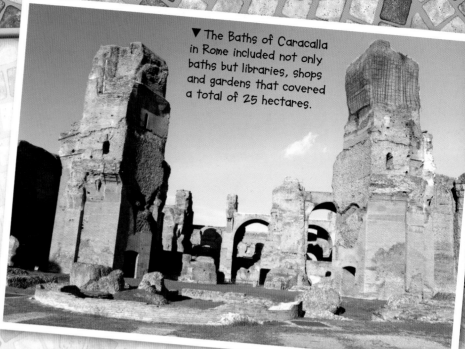

▼ The Baths of Caracalla in Rome included not only baths but libraries, shops and gardens that covered a total of 25 hectares.

② *Tepidarium*
Cool or tepid pool

① *Caldarium*
Hot room

③ *Frigidarium*
Coldest pool

Fires heat the water for the hot rooms

▲ Roman baths were open to anyone who paid the entrance fee. They were one of the few areas where rich and poor mixed freely. Some baths had two sections, one for men and one for women, but most baths had days for men and days for women.

153

Having fun

343 Roman theatre-goers preferred comedies to tragedies. Comic plays had happy endings, and made audiences laugh. Tragedies were serious, and ended with misery and suffering. The Romans also liked clowns, and invented mime, a story told without words, through dance and movement.

▼ All the parts in Roman plays were performed by men. For women's roles, men wore masks and dressed in female costume. Women could not be actors, except in mime.

Stages were backed by permanent walls of stone with doorways and balconies that could be used to represent temples and houses

The front of the stage was called the *pulpitum*. Actors stood here to make important speeches

Theatres had no roofs, so audiences were not undercover. Plays took place only during the day when there was enough light

QUIZ

1. What is the name for a story told through dance and music without words?

2. Why did some Roman politicians give away free tickets to plays?

3. How many people could be seated in the Roman theatre at Orange in France?

344 Plays were originally part of religious festivals. Many dramas showed scenes from myths and legends, and were designed to make people think about morals. Later, plays were written on all sorts of topics — including politics. Some were paid for by rich politicians, to spread their message. They gave free tickets to Roman citizens, hoping to win votes.

Answers:
1. Mime 2. In the hope of winning votes 3. 10,000

345 Theatres were huge and well-built.

The theatre at Orange in France seats almost 10,000 people and is so cleverly designed that even people in the back row can hear the actors.

Seats were made of hard stone, but sometimes people could hire soft cushions to sit on

346 Actors wore masks to help audiences see what each character was feeling.

They were carved and painted in bright colours, with large features and exaggerated expressions of happiness, sadness or fright.

347 The Romans liked music and dancing.

Groups of buskers played in the streets, or could be hired for parties. Among ordinary families, favourite instruments included pipes, castanets, flutes, cymbals and horns. Rich, educated people preferred the gentler sound of the lyre, which was played to accompany poets and singers.

348 People enjoyed games of skill and chance.

Adults and children played dice and knucklebones. They played a game similar to draughts, which relied on luck and quick thinking. Sometimes bets were made on who would win.

▶ Six-sided dice were made of bone or ivory. They were shaken in a round pot before being thrown.

◄ Masks worn by Roman actors as shown in a mosaic from Rome. The male mask was used for comedy, the female for tragedy.

349 **Gladiators were admired for their strength, skill and bravery.** These men were sent into an arena (an open space with tiered seats on all sides) to fight. Most gladiators would be killed or badly injured in the arena.

▶ Different types of gladiator had special equipment and fought in ways governed by strict rules, which were enforced by a referee.

Secutor

Samnite

Hoplomachus

350 **Most gladiators didn't choose to fight.** They were prisoners of war or criminals condemned to fight in the arena. Some men volunteered as gladiators to gain fame and wealth. Success could bring riches and freedom.

I DON'T BELIEVE IT!

Some gladiators became so popular that people used to write graffiti about them on the walls of buildings around Rome!

351 **Gladiators fought wild beasts.** Animals such as lions, tigers and crocodiles were brought from distant parts of the Empire to be hunted in the arena. Sometimes criminals with no weapons were put into the arena with the wild animals. They did not last long.

352 **The Colosseum was an amazing building for its time.** Also known as the Flavian Amphitheatre, it was a huge oval arena in the centre of Rome, used for gladiator fights and the executions of criminals. It opened in AD 80, and could seat 50,000 people. It was built of stone, concrete and marble and had 80 separate entrances.

▼ The Colosseum was the largest amphitheatre in the Roman empire.

▶ Chariot drivers wore helmets, but no other protective clothing.

354 **Chariots often collided and overturned.** Each charioteer carried a sharp knife, called a *falx*, to cut himself free from the wreckage. Even so, many horses and charioteers were killed.

353 **Some Romans liked a day at the races.** Horses pulled fast chariots round racetracks, called 'circuses'. The most famous was the Circus Maximus in Rome, which could hold 250,000 spectators. There could be up to 24 races each day. Twelve chariots took part in each race, running seven times round the oval track – a total distance of about 8 kilometres.

355 **Racing rivalries sometimes led to riots.** Races were organized by four separate teams – the Reds, Blues, Greens and Whites. Charioteers wore tunics in their team colours. Each team had a keen – and violent – group of fans.

Ruling Rome

▼ Caesar's power and ambition angered his political opponents, and a group of them assassinated him.

356 According to legend, the first king, Romulus, came to power in 753 BC. Six kings ruled after him, but they were unjust and cruel. After King Tarquin the Proud was overthrown in 509 BC Rome became a republic (a state without a king). Every year the people elected two consuls (senior lawyers) to head the government. Other officials were elected too. The republic lasted for over 400 years.

357 In 47 BC a successful general called Julius Caesar declared himself dictator. This meant that he wanted to rule on his own for life. Many people feared that he was trying to end the republic, and rule like the old kings. Caesar was murdered in 44 BC by his political enemies. After this, there were many years of civil war.

▲ Legend says the twins Romulus and Remus were suckled by a wolf before being rescued by a shepherd.

I DON'T BELIEVE IT!

Some Roman emperors were mad and even dangerous. Emperor Nero was said to have laughed and played music while watching a terrible fire that destroyed a large part of Rome.

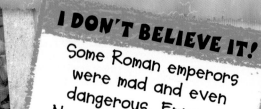

▲ This relief shows the emperor Trajan speaking to his army in AD 106. By this date emperors would command the army in battle and were expected to be talented generals.

358

In 27 BC Caesar's nephew Octavian seized power in Rome. He declared himself 'First Citizen', and said he would bring back peace and good government to Rome. He ended the civil war, and introduced many strong new laws. But he also changed the Roman government forever. He took a new name, 'Augustus', and became the first emperor of Rome.

359

Later the army took over. In 193 Emperor Commodus was murdered and the senate met to decide who would take over. The army marched to Rome and made Septimus Severus emperor. After this it was the army who decided who would be emperor.

Emperor Nero
AD 37–68

Emperor Caligula
AD 12–41

Emperor Constantine
280–337

◄ The emperors put their portraits on coins to remind everyone who was in charge of the empire.

◄ The Roman general Octavian Caesar ruled Rome from 27 BC to AD 14.

In the army

360
Being a soldier was a good career, if you didn't get killed! Roman soldiers were well paid and cared for. The empire needed troops to defend its land against attack, and soldiers were well trained. Good fighters were promoted and received extra pay. When they retired they were given money or land.

361
Roman troops carried three main weapons. They fought with javelins, swords and daggers. Each man had to buy his own set, and look after them carefully – one day, his life might depend on them.

◄ Roman soldiers used the *gladius*, a stabbing sword about 80 centimetres long.

362
Soldiers needed many skills. On arrival at a new base they set up camps of tents, but soon afterwards built permanent forts defended by strong walls. Each legion contained men with a wide range of skills, such as cooks, builders, doctors, carpenters, blacksmiths and engineers – but they all had to fight!

▶ Soldiers used their shields to make a protective shell called a *testudo*, or 'tortoise'.

◄ The ballista was a weapon that could hurl a heavy javelin accurately over a range of 500 metres.

363 **The army could march up to 30 kilometres in a day.** When they were hurrying to put down a rebellion, or moving from fort to fort, soldiers travelled quickly, on foot. Troops marched along straight, well-made army roads. Each soldier had to carry a heavy pack containing weapons, armour, tools, cooking pots, food and spare clothes.

364 **The army contained citizens and 'helpers'.** Roman citizens joined the regular army. Men who were not citizens could also fight for Rome. They were known as auxiliaries (helpers) and were organized into special units of their own.

I DON'T BELIEVE IT!

Roman soldiers guarding the cold northern frontiers of Britain kept warm by wearing short woollen trousers – like underpants – beneath their tunics!

◄ Roman cavalry were usually auxiliary troops raised from non-Roman peoples.

365 **Soldiers worshipped their own special god.** At forts and army camps, soldiers built temples where they honoured the god Mithras, who they believed protected them and gave them life after death.

Ruled by Rome

366 **More than 50 million people were ruled by Rome.** Celts, Germans, Iberians, and many other peoples lived in territories held by Rome's armies. They had their own languages, customs and beliefs. Rome sent governors to force conquered peoples to pay Roman taxes and obey Roman laws.

▼ The Roman city of Londinium (London) was built where a bridge could be built over the wide River Thames.

367 **A few conquered kings and queens did not accept Roman rule.** In AD 60 Boudicca, queen of the Iceni tribe of eastern England, led a rebellion against the Romans in Britain. Her army marched on London and other cities but was defeated by Roman soldiers.

▼ British warriors led by Queen Boudicca destroyed London and killed everyone they found.

LOOK LIKE A CELTIC WARRIOR!

Roman writers reported how Celtic warriors decorated their faces and bodies with patterns before going into battle. They believed that the paint was magic, and would protect them. The Celts used a deep-blue dye made from a plant called woad. Ask an adult if you have some special face-painting make-up, then try using it to make up some scary war-paint designs of your own.

368 Cleopatra used beauty and charm to stop the Romans invading. Cleopatra was queen of Egypt and she knew that the Egyptian army would not be able to defeat Roman soldiers. Two Roman army generals, Julius Caesar and Mark Antony, fell in love with Cleopatra. She prevented the Romans invading for many years, but Egypt was eventually conquered.

▶ Queen Cleopatra shown wearing the traditional clothing of an Egyptian queen.

369 Romans built monuments to celebrate their victories. Trajan, who ruled from AD 98–117, was a Roman soldier who became emperor. After his army conquered Dacia (now Romania) in AD 106, he gave orders for a 30-metre-high stone pillar to be built in the Forum in Rome. The pillar was decorated with carvings of 2500 Roman soldiers winning wars. It still stands today and is known as Trajan's Column.

▼ This map shows the Roman Empire in brown, and the roads that they built in black.

The farming life

370 **Rome relied on farmers.** Most Romans lived in the countryside and worked on farms. Farmers produced food for city-dwellers. Food was grown on big estates by teams of slaves, and on small peasant farms where single families worked together.

371 **Farm produce was imported from all over the empire.** Wool and honey came from Britain, wine from Greece, and 400,000 tonnes of wheat were shipped across the Mediterranean Sea from Egypt every year. It was ground into flour, which was used to make bread, the Romans' basic food.

▼ A relief showing a merchant taking delivery of large pottery amphorae (tall jugs or jars) filled with oil or wine.

▲ Slaves work the land on a large Roman estate.

372 **Roman grapes grew on trees.** Vines (climbing plants that produce grapes) were planted among fruit trees in orchards. The trees provided support for the vine stems, and welcome shade to stop the grapes getting scorched by the sun. Grapes were one of the most important crops on Roman farms. The ripe fruits were picked and dried to become raisins, or pulped and made into wine.

KEY

1. Beehives for honey
2. Treading grapes for wine
3. Owner of the farm
4. Vineyard and orchard
5. Threshing wheat
6. Sheep kept in fields
7. Pressing olives
8. Farmworkers harvesting grain
9. Vegetable patch

373

The most valuable fruit was small, hard, green and bitter! Olives could be pickled in salty water to eat with bread and cheese, or crushed to provide oil. The Romans used olive oil as a medicine, for cooking and preserving food, for cleaning and softening the skin, and even for burning in lamps.

374

Farmers didn't have machines to help them. Heavy work was done by animals or humans, and ploughs were pulled by oxen. Crops were harvested by men and women using sickles (curved knives) and loaded onto carts by hand. Donkeys turned mill wheels to crush olives, grind grain, and to raise drinking water from wells.

▶ This mosaic shows dates being harvested.

TRUE OR FALSE?

1. The Romans imported wool and honey from Britain.

2. A raisin is a dried olive.

3. The Romans used olive oil as a medicine.

Answers:
1. True 2. False 3. True

165

Work like a slave

375 In Rome not all people were equal. How you were treated in society depended on your class. Free-born people (citizens) had rights that were guaranteed by law – for example, to travel or find work. Citizens could vote in elections, and receive free food handouts. Slaves had very few rights. They belonged to their owners just like dogs or horses.

376 Slaves were purchased from slave-traders or born to slave parents. People could also be condemned to slavery as a punishment for a serious crime, or if they were captured in a war.

▼ Slaves were bought and sold at slave-markets. They were paraded before the citizens to be chosen or rejected. The slaves could not leave, or choose what work to do. They could be cruelly punished, neglected or given away.

▼ Slaves at work in a Roman mosaic from about the year AD 500. They were expected to wear simple tunics.

377
Slaves were trained to do all sorts of tasks. They did everything their owners demanded, from looking after children to hard labour on farms. Many slaves were trusted by their owners, who valued their skills. A few slaves became respected chefs or doctors.

378
Sometimes slaves were set free by their owners. Freedom could be a reward for loyalty or long service. Some sick or dying slave-owners gave orders that their slaves should be freed. They did not want their slaves to pass to a new owner who might treat them badly.

379
Some slaves did very well after they were freed. Former slaves used the skills they had learned to set up businesses of their own. Many were successful, and a few became very rich.

Roman know-how

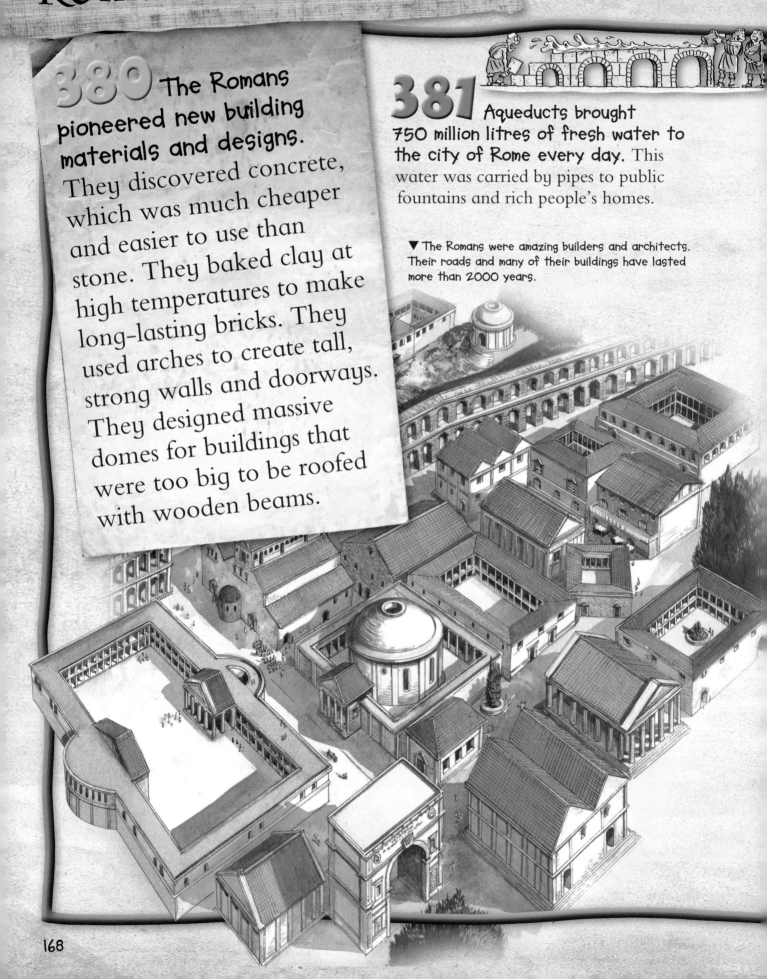

380 The Romans pioneered new building materials and designs. They discovered concrete, which was much cheaper and easier to use than stone. They baked clay at high temperatures to make long-lasting bricks. They used arches to create tall, strong walls and doorways. They designed massive domes for buildings that were too big to be roofed with wooden beams.

381 Aqueducts brought 750 million litres of fresh water to the city of Rome every day. This water was carried by pipes to public fountains and rich people's homes.

▼ The Romans were amazing builders and architects. Their roads and many of their buildings have lasted more than 2000 years.

Our word 'plumber' comes from plumbum, the Latin word for the lead used by Romans to make water pipes. The same word is also used for a 'plumb-line', still in use today.

◀ Romans used valves to pump water uphill. Water would then come out of fountains.

384 Even the best doctors often failed to cure their patients. But Roman doctors were skilled at sewing up cuts and joining broken bones. They also used herbs for medicines and painkillers.

382 No one improved on the Roman's water supplies until the 1800s! They invented pumps with valves to pump water uphill. This went into high tanks above fountains. Gravity pulled the water out of the fountain's spout.

383 Despite their advanced technology, Romans believed that illness was caused by witchcraft. To find a cure, they made a special visit to a temple, to ask the gods with healing powers to make them better.

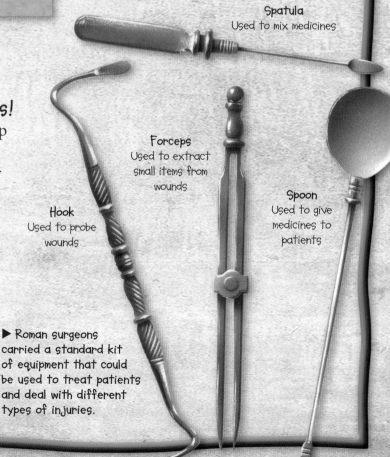

Spatula
Used to mix medicines

Forceps
Used to extract small items from wounds

Hook
Used to probe wounds

Spoon
Used to give medicines to patients

▶ Roman surgeons carried a standard kit of equipment that could be used to treat patients and deal with different types of injuries.

Prayers and sacrifices

▼ The marriage of Jupiter and Juno, watched by Roma the patron goddess of the city of Rome.

Juno
Queen of the gods and patron of marriage

Jupiter
King of the gods and god of the sky

Minerva
Goddess of the arts and of wisdom, daughter of Jupiter

Neptune
God of rivers, the sea and earthquakes, brother of Jupiter

Mars
God of warfare and peace treaties, ancestor of the Roman people

Venus
Represented love and beauty, like the Greek goddess Aphrodite

Apollo
Greek god of arts, light and prophecy, worshipped in Rome from 430 BC

Diana
Goddess of hunting, the moon and childbirth, daughter of Jupiter

Vulcan
God of fire and blacksmiths, husband of Venus, son of Jupiter

Vesta
Goddess of home and family, her temple had an eternal flame

Mercury
God of business, money and travel, messenger of the gods

Ceres
Goddess of grain crops and farmers, sister of Jupiter

385 **The Romans had many gods.** There were gods of the city, the country, and of the underworld, and some were worshipped by people of certain professions. The Romans even adopted gods from other countries that were part of the empire. Ideas and gods from Greece had a very big impact.

386 **The emperor was also chief priest.** As part of his duties he said prayers and offered sacrifices to the gods who protected Rome. His title was *pontifex maximus* (chief bridge-builder) because people believed he acted as a bridge between the gods and ordinary people.

I DON'T BELIEVE IT!

After an animal had been sacrificed to the gods, a priest, called a *haruspex*, examined its liver. If it was diseased, bad luck was on the way!

387

Families made offerings to the gods every day. They left food, wine and incense in front of a shrine in their house. A shrine is like a mini temple. It contained statues of ancient gods called the *lares* and *penates*. The *lares* were ancestor spirits who looked after living family members. The *penates* guarded the family's food.

▲ A Roman pours a libation (small offering) to the gods, onto the ground at a temple.

388

Romans were superstitious. They decorated their homes with magic symbols, and children were made to wear good-luck charms. They thought they could foretell the future by observing animals – bees were a sign of riches but a hooting owl foretold danger.

389

Some of the first Christians lived in Rome. For years Christianity was banned in Rome, so Christians met secretly in catacombs (underground passages). They also used the catacombs as burial places. The persecution of Christians ended after 313, and in 380 Christianity became the official state religion of Rome.

On the move

390 Rome was at the hub of a network of roads that stretched for more than 85,000 kilometres. It had been built to link outlying parts of the empire to the capital, so that Roman armies or government officials could travel quickly. To make travel as quick as possible, roads were built in straight lines, taking the shortest route.

▲ A street in Pompeii. The stepping stones were provided so people could cross without treading in horse droppings and rubbish.

392 Some Roman roads have survived for over 2000 years. Each road was made of layers of earth and stones on top of a firm, flat foundation. It was surfaced with stone slabs or gravel. The centre had a camber (curved surface), so that rainwater drained away into ditches on either side.

391 Rome's first main road was built in 312 BC. Its name was the Via Appia (*via* is the Latin word for 'road'). It ran from Rome to the port of Brundisium on the south-east coast of Italy. Many travellers from Greece arrived there, and the new road made their journey to Rome quicker and easier.

▶ Trained men worked out the route, and slaves did the heavy labour. Army roads were built by soldiers.

Route accurately marked out

Solid foundations

Drainage ditch

Large surface slabs

393 **Engineers used special tools to help them make accurate surveys.** They made careful plans and took measurements before starting any building project, such as a new road or city walls.

▼ These engineers are using a *groma* to measure straight lines on a road.

394 **Poor people walked everywhere.** They couldn't afford to hire a horse or donkey, or a carriage pulled by oxen. With luck they could hitch a lift in a farm wagon – but it wouldn't be a comfortable ride!

395 **Town streets were crowded and dirty.** Rich people travelled in curtained beds called litters, carried by slaves. Stepping stones allowed ordinary people to avoid the mud and rubbish underfoot.

396 **Heavy loads often travelled by water.** There were no lorries in Roman times. Ships, powered by sails and by slaves rowing, carried people and cargo over water. But water-transport was slow, and could be dangerous. Roman ships were often attacked by pirates, and shipwrecks were common.

◄ A Roman war galley. The ram at the bow could be used to sink enemy ships, or the soldiers might fight their way on board enemy ships.

Uncovering the past

397 Lots of evidence survives to tell us about Roman times. Archaeologists have discovered the remains of many Roman buildings, from palaces and aqueducts, to temples, hospitals and homes. They have also found works of art, coins, jewellery, pottery, glass, and many tools and objects used in daily life.

398 The oceans contain secrets from the past. Marine archaeology is the hunt for amazing relics under the sea. Many Roman shipwrecks have been discovered in the Mediterranean Sea, including a wine carrier with 6000 amphorae off the coast near Marseilles in France.

▼ Archaeologists find a Roman pot in the bed of the Ljubljanica River in Slovenia. Underwater techniques are relatively new and have allowed archaeologists to make dramatic discoveries.

▼ A mosaic preserved at Herculaneum shows Roman gods.

▼ Roman coins have survived in large numbers allowing us to study emperors and gods.

QUIZ

1. What does the name Marcus mean?
2. Which of these things would not be discovered by an archaeologist studying ancient Rome: glass, telephone, coin?
3. What is marine archaeology?

Answers:
1. God of War 2. A telephone 3. The study of relics underwater

399 Until the 20th century, grand, important buildings were often planned and decorated in Roman style. Architects believed that Roman designs inspired respect, so many cities have churches, museums, art galleries, colleges and even banks that look like Roman temples or Roman villas.

400 Roman names are still quite common. In some parts of the world, children are given Roman names or names based on Latin words. These include Amanda (Loveable), Diana (Moon Goddess), Patricia (Noble), Laura (Laurel-tree), Marcus (God of War), Victor (Winner), and Vincent (Conqueror).

▲ Casts of bodies found in Pompeii. The casts are made by pouring plaster into hollow spaces left in the volcanic ash where bodies have rotted away.

GLADIATORS

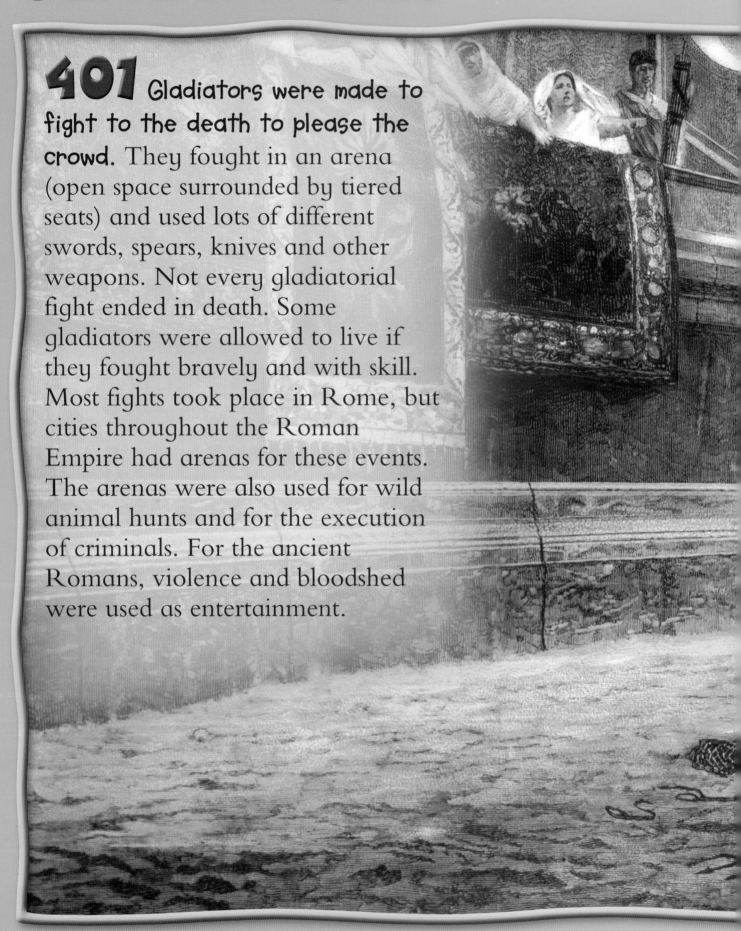

401 **Gladiators were made to fight to the death to please the crowd.** They fought in an arena (open space surrounded by tiered seats) and used lots of different swords, spears, knives and other weapons. Not every gladiatorial fight ended in death. Some gladiators were allowed to live if they fought bravely and with skill. Most fights took place in Rome, but cities throughout the Roman Empire had arenas for these events. The arenas were also used for wild animal hunts and for the execution of criminals. For the ancient Romans, violence and bloodshed were used as entertainment.

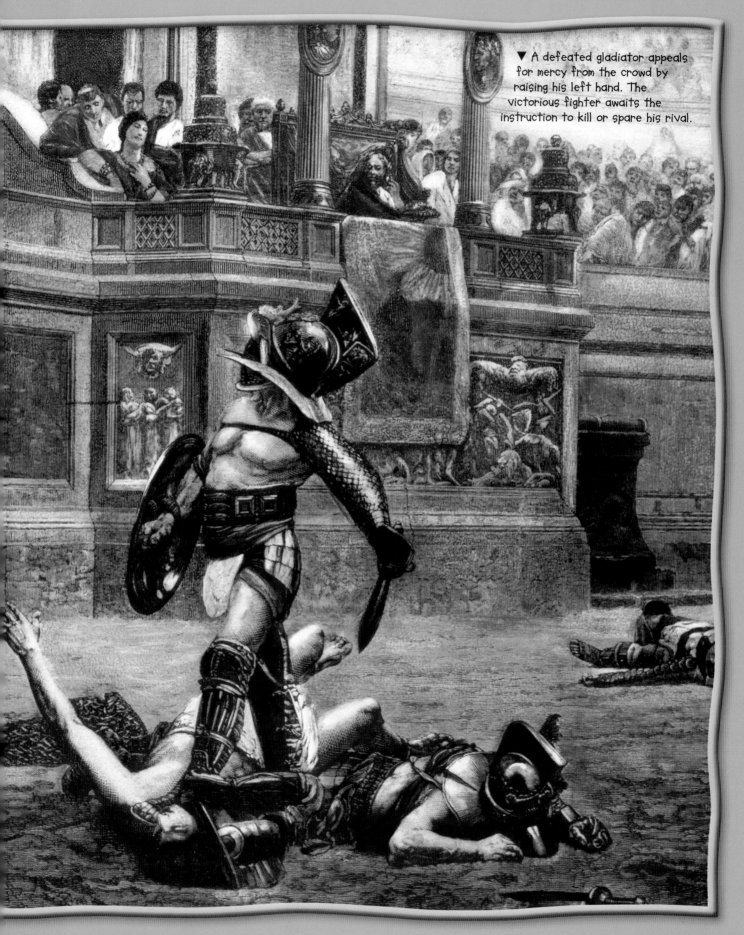

▼ A defeated gladiator appeals for mercy from the crowd by raising his left hand. The victorious fighter awaits the instruction to kill or spare his rival.

The first gladiators

402 **The first gladiators were not from Rome.** The Romans did not invent the idea of gladiators. They believed the idea of men fighting in an arena probably came to Rome from the region of Etruria. But the first proper gladiators probably came from Campania, an area of Italy south of Rome.

▲ The city of Rome began as a small town between Etruria and Campania in central Italy.

403 **The first Roman gladiators fought in 264 BC.** Six slaves were set to fight each other with swords, but they were not allowed to wear any armour. The fights did not last for long before one of the slaves in each pair was killed.

▶ The gladius was the standard weapon used by early gladiators. It was kept in a sheath called a scabbard.

178

404 **The first gladiatorial fights were always part of a funeral.** The name for a gladiatorial show, a munus, means a duty owed to the dead. The first fights were held at the funerals of politicians and noblemen, who ordered the games in their wills.

▶ The first gladiators were usually elderly slaves or troublemakers, who would not be missed by their owners.

405 **In early funeral games, food was more important than gladiators.** The Romans used funerals to show off how wealthy and important they were. Free food and drink were laid out at the funeral for any Roman citizen who wanted to come along. Gifts of money, jewellery and clothing were also handed out. The family of the person being buried would wear their finest clothes. The first gladiator fights were just one part of the whole funeral.

406 **Gladiators were named after their weapons.** The word gladiator means 'a man who uses a gladius'. The gladius was a type of short, stabbing sword that was used by Roman soldiers. It was about 40 centimetres long and had a very sharp point. It was generally used for slashing, not for cutting.

Not all gladiators used the gladius, but the name was used for all fighters in the arena.

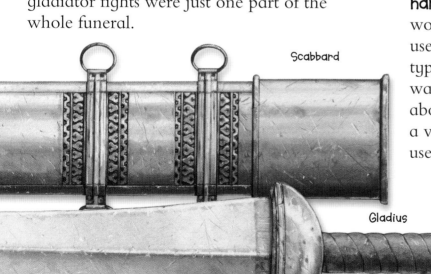

Scabbard

Gladius

Prisoners of war

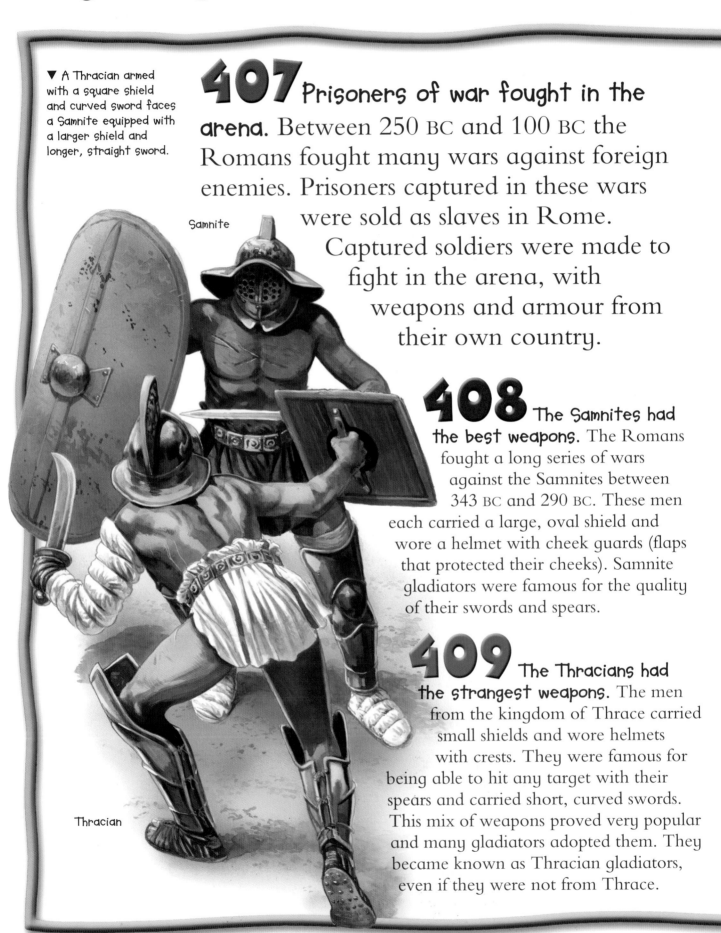

▼ A Thracian armed with a square shield and curved sword faces a Samnite equipped with a larger shield and longer, straight sword.

Samnite

Thracian

407 **Prisoners of war fought in the arena.** Between 250 BC and 100 BC the Romans fought many wars against foreign enemies. Prisoners captured in these wars were sold as slaves in Rome. Captured soldiers were made to fight in the arena, with weapons and armour from their own country.

408 The Samnites had the best weapons. The Romans fought a long series of wars against the Samnites between 343 BC and 290 BC. These men each carried a large, oval shield and wore a helmet with cheek guards (flaps that protected their cheeks). Samnite gladiators were famous for the quality of their swords and spears.

409 The Thracians had the strangest weapons. The men from the kingdom of Thrace carried small shields and wore helmets with crests. They were famous for being able to hit any target with their spears and carried short, curved swords. This mix of weapons proved very popular and many gladiators adopted them. They became known as Thracian gladiators, even if they were not from Thrace.

▶ The tall, fair-skinned Celts decorated their bodies and shields with bright colours.

410 Celts painted their bodies before going into battle. The Celts were the only people to have captured Rome, in 390 BC. They lived in northern Italy and across Europe. The Romans forced many Celtic prisoners to fight in their native clothes and with native weapons.

◀ The Numidians from North Africa were famous for their skill on horseback. They often fought in the arena using light javelins.

411 The Numidians fought on horseback. Numidia was an area of northern Africa in what is now Algeria. The area was famous for breeding quality horses and its army included large numbers of cavalry (soldiers on horseback). Prisoners of war from Numidia rode horses when they appeared in the arena.

Gladiators and politics

▲ A person's ashes were stored in a pot or urn until the funeral.

412 Funerals were delayed for years. Gladiatorial shows were organized as part of the funerals of rich and powerful noblemen. However, the heir of the man who had died would want to hold the show when he was standing for election so that he could impress the voters.

413 A good gladiator show could win an election. In ancient Rome, votes were not cast in secret. Each voter had to give his name to an official called a censor and then declare how he was voting. The men standing for election stood near the censor to see how people voted. Putting on an impressive gladiator show could gain votes.

▼ A citizen waiting to vote at an election. The censor kept a list of everyone entitled to vote and people had to prove who they were before voting.

I DON'T BELIEVE IT!

In 165 BC, a play was interrupted when the entire audience left the theatre to watch a gladiatorial show. The actors were left alone in the theatre!

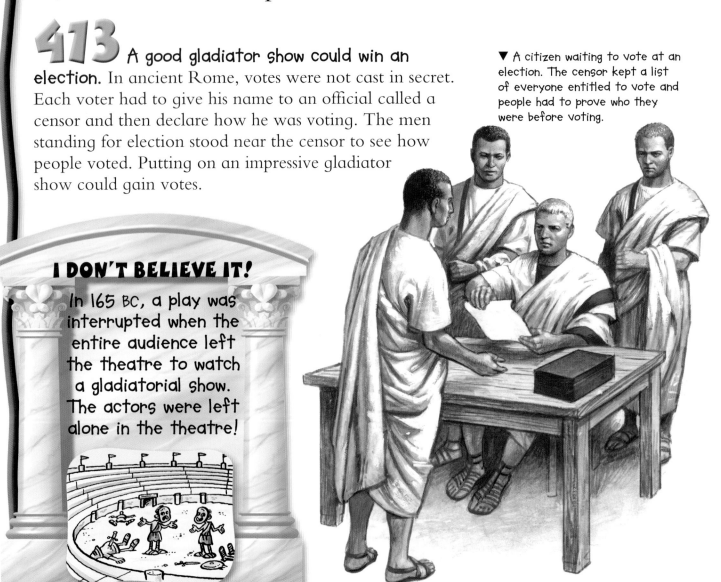

414 **Some politicians hired gangs of gladiators to beat up their opponents.** If a citizen could not be persuaded, by gladiator shows or the payment of money, to vote for a certain candidate, the candidate might use gladiators to bully him. Gladiators were armed with clubs and given the names of citizens who should be threatened. Every election was accompanied by this sort of violence.

▲ Men were posted at the entrance to the arena to ensure that only voters entered.

415 **Only voters could watch the games.** The purpose of holding spectacular gladiatorial shows was to influence voters. Only citizens of Rome could vote, so only they were allowed to attend the shows. Citizens who were known to be voting for an opponent were turned away, as were slaves and foreigners who could not vote.

416 **The best seats went to men who donated money to the election campaign.** Standing for an election cost a lot of money in ancient Rome. Rich men would give or lend money to the candidate they preferred. In return they would get the best seats in a gladiatorial show and would expect to receive titles or government money if their candidate won.

◀ Roman coins were made of gold, silver or bronze and carried a portrait of the emperor on one side.

Spartacus!

417 The most famous gladiator of all was Spartacus. He led a rebellion of gladiators and other slaves in the year 73 BC. At first Spartacus had just 70 gladiators with him, but later over 40,000 runaway slaves joined his forces.

418 Spartacus was a gladiator from the kingdom of Thrace. He joined the Roman army, but did not like it and tried to run away. As a punishment, Spartacus was sent to train as a gladiator, although he was allowed to take his wife with him.

419 The gladiators, led by Spartacus, defeated the Roman army. After breaking out of the gladiator school (called a ludus), Spartacus hid on the slopes of Mount Vesuvius, near Naples. He defeated a small Roman force sent to capture him and then led his growing army to northern Italy. There, at Modena, he defeated a large Roman army and stole valuable goods.

420 Spartacus wanted to cross the Alps, a large mountain range. After winning the battle at Modena, Spartacus wanted to return to Thrace. However, his men wanted to raid cities. They made Spartacus lead them back to southern Italy.

421 The wrong general was credited for defeating Spartacus. Spartacus and his army of slaves and gladiators were defeated by a new Roman army at Lucania. This army was commanded by Marcus Licinius Crassus. One small group of slaves fled the battle and was captured by a commander named Gnaeus Pompey. He then rode to Rome and announced that he had defeated the rebels.

◀ The 1960 movie *Spartacus* starred Kirk Douglas (centre) as the escaped gladiator. Spartacus equipped his army of gladiators and slaves with weapons stolen from the Romans.

Caesar's games

422 **Julius Caesar borrowed money to buy his gladiators.** Caesar rose to become the ruler of the Roman Empire. Early in his career he staged spectacular games to win votes in elections. But Caesar was too poor to afford to pay the bills, so he borrowed money from richer men. When he won the elections, Caesar repaid the men with favours and titles.

▲ Julius Caesar (102–44 BC) was a politician who won several elections after staging magnificent games to entertain the voters.

◀ War elephants were popular attractions, and gladiators were specially trained in how to fight against them.

423 **Caesar's gladiators fought in silver armour.** In 65 BC, Julius Caesar staged the funeral games for his father, who had died 20 years earlier. Caesar was standing for election to be chief priest of Rome. To make his games even more special, Caesar dressed his 640 gladiators in armour made of solid silver.

424 **Caesar brought war elephants to Rome.** In 46 BC Julius Caesar celebrated a victory in North Africa by staging gladiatorial games in Rome. Among the prisoners of war forced to fight in the arena were 40 war elephants, together with the men trained to fight them.

425 **Caesar turned senators (governors of Rome) into gladiators.** On one occasion Caesar forced two rich noblemen to fight in the arena. They had been sentenced to death by a court, but Caesar ordered that the man who killed the other in the arena could go free.

426 **Caesar's final show was too big for the arena.** The games staged by Julius Caesar when he wanted to become dictator of Rome were the grandest ever held. After weeks of shows and feasts, the final day saw a fight between two armies of 500 infantry (foot soldiers) and 30 cavalry. The battle was so large it had to be held in the enormous chariot race course, Circus Maximus.

QUIZ

1. Did Caesar's gladiators wear armour made of silver, gold or bronze?
2. Was Caesar's final show a big or small show?
3. Where did Caesar get the money to buy gladiators?

Answers:
1. Silver. 2. It was a big show.
3. He borrowed money from richer men.

▼ Chariot racing was a hugely popular sport that thrilled the crowds in ancient Rome.

The mob

427 **The Roman mob could overpower emperors.** Over a million people lived in ancient Rome. Many were voting citizens who did not have regular jobs. Even the most powerful emperors had to keep this vast mob of Romans happy. If an emperor did not put on impressive gladiatorial shows he could be booed, attacked or even killed.

▲ Emperor Vitellius (AD 69) was murdered by a mob of Romans after failing to put on any impressive games.

◀ The seats in the arena were numbered and cushions were sometimes provided for extra comfort.

428 **Each seat was saved for a particular person.** People attending the gladiator games had their own seats. The row and seat number were written on small clay tablets that were handed out by the organizer of the games. Some seats were given to whoever queued up outside the arena.

429 Women in ancient Rome could not vote, so they were given seats at the back of the crowd. The best seats were reserved for the men who could vote and had money to help the editor (the man who staged gladiatorial games).

◀ A wounded gladiator pleads for his life by raising the first finger of his left hand. The thumbs-down signal from the mob indicates that he should die.

430 The mob decided which gladiators lived, and which died. A wounded gladiator could appeal for mercy by holding up the first finger of his left hand. The mob gave a thumbs-down gesture if they thought the gladiator should die, or hid their thumbs in clenched fists if they thought he should live. The editor usually did what the mob wanted because he wanted them to vote for him.

I DON'T BELIEVE IT!

Poor Roman citizens were given free bread by the government. In one month in 44 BC, more than 330,000 men queued up to receive this free handout of food.

Amazing arenas

431 **The first gladiator fights took place in the cattle market.** The cattle market, or Forum Boarium, was a large open space by the river Tiber. Cattle pens were cleared away to make space for fighting, while the audience watched from shops and temples.

◀ The crowd watched early gladiatorial fights in the cattle market from shops and pavements.

432 **Most fights took place in the Forum.** This was the largest open square in the centre of Rome. The most important temples and government buildings stood around the Forum. After about 150 BC, gladiatorial games were held in the Forum and temporary wooden stands were erected in which spectators could sit.

433 **One fight took place in a swivelling arena.** In 53 BC, the politician Gaius Scribonius Curio put on a gladiator show and impressed the crowd by staging two plays in back-to-back theatres. The theatres swivelled around to form an arena for a small gladiator show. The crowd loved the new idea and Curio went on to win several elections.

434 The first purpose-built arena had the emperor's name carved on it. In 29 BC an amphitheatre (an open-air building with rows of seats, one above the other) was built to the north of Rome by the politician Titus Statilius Taurus. The amphitheatre was built of stone and timber to replace temporary wooden stands in the Forum. Taurus wanted to impress Emperor Augustus so he carved the name 'Augustus' over the entrance.

▼ The name Augustus dominated the entrance to the arena built by Taurus.

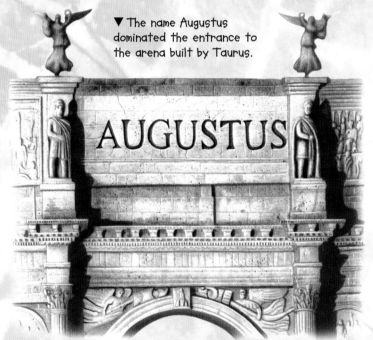

435 Every arena had the same layout. Arenas were oval with an entrance at each end. The gladiators came into the arena through one entrance, and the other was reserved for servants and for carrying out any dead gladiators. The editor sat in a special section of the seating called the tribunal editoris, which was on the north side in the shade.

▼ All gladiatorial stadiums were oval in shape, with blocks of seating rising from the central arena.

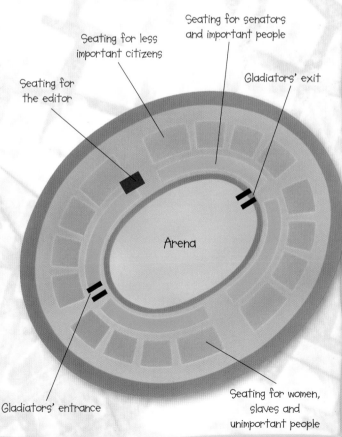

Seating for less important citizens

Seating for senators and important people

Gladiators' exit

Seating for the editor

Arena

Gladiators' entrance

Seating for women, slaves and unimportant people

The mighty Colosseum

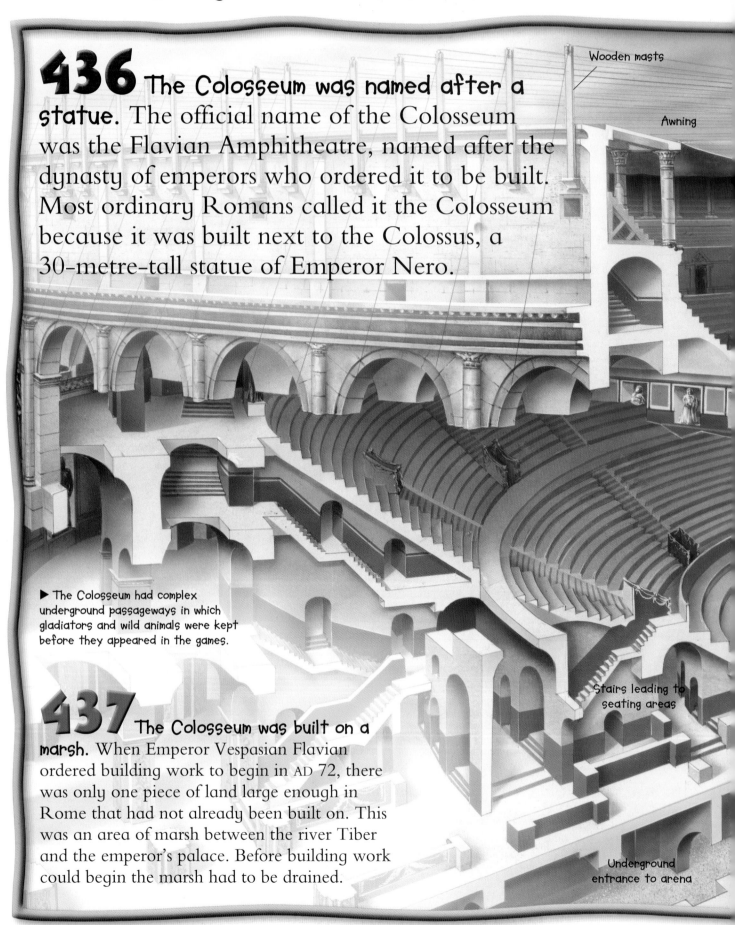

436 **The Colosseum was named after a statue.** The official name of the Colosseum was the Flavian Amphitheatre, named after the dynasty of emperors who ordered it to be built. Most ordinary Romans called it the Colosseum because it was built next to the Colossus, a 30-metre-tall statue of Emperor Nero.

Wooden masts

Awning

► The Colosseum had complex underground passageways in which gladiators and wild animals were kept before they appeared in the games.

437 **The Colosseum was built on a marsh.** When Emperor Vespasian Flavian ordered building work to begin in AD 72, there was only one piece of land large enough in Rome that had not already been built on. This was an area of marsh between the river Tiber and the emperor's palace. Before building work could begin the marsh had to be drained.

Stairs leading to seating areas

Underground entrance to arena

438 **The Colosseum could seat 50,000 spectators.** The huge seating area was divided into over 80 sections. Each section had a door and flight of steps that led to the outside of the Colosseum. The standing room at the top was reserved for slaves and may have held another 4000 people.

439 **The Colosseum was probably the largest building in the world.** The outer walls stood 46 metres tall and covered an area 194 metres long by 160 metres wide. The walls were covered in stone, but the structure was made of brick or concrete.

440 **The first games in the Colosseum lasted 100 days.** The Colosseum was finished in AD 80, during the reign of Emperor Titus. He wanted to show that he was the most generous man ever to live in Rome, so he organized gladiatorial games to last for 100 days. Thousands of gladiators and animals fought in these games.

Tiered seating

Trapdoors

Arena floor

Network of corridors and machinery beneath arena floor

Who were the gladiators?

441 **Gladiators were divided into types based on their weapons.** Not all gladiators used the same weapons or fought in the same way. Some gladiators fought with weapons that had been popular in other countries or were used by different types of soldiers. Others used weapons and armour that were made especially for the arena.

442 **Murmillo gladiators used army weapons and military armour.** Their shields and swords were similar to those used by infantry in the Roman army. The shield was one metre long and 65 centimetres wide. The sword was used for stabbing, not cutting.

443 **Thracian gladiators used lightweight armour.** The weapons of the Thracians were based on those used by soldiers from the kingdom of Thrace. The shield was small and square and the leg armour had long metal guards. The sword had a curved blade and the helmets were decorated with a griffin's head (a griffin was an imaginary bird).

Murmillo

Thracian

◀ ▲ ▶ Thracian, Murmillo and Provocator gladiators were all equipped with armour and heavy weapons. They usually fought each other, sometimes in teams. The lightly equipped Retiarius only had a net and trident.

444 Provocator gladiators wore the heaviest armour of all gladiators. They had a breastplate that protected the chest, a round helmet and leg armour that reached above the knees. The shield was about 80 centimetres long and 60 centimetres wide. They used a short, stabbing sword with a straight blade.

Retiarius

Provocator

MAKE A SHIELD

You will need:
cardboard   scissors
string   coloured paints

1. Take the sheet of cardboard and cut out a rectangular shape with rounded corners.

2. Ask an adult to make a pair of holes close to each long side and tie string through them to make handles.

3. Paint the front of the shield with a bright, colourful design.

445 Retiarius gladiators had a fishing net and trident. These gladiators wore very little armour. They relied on speed and skill to escape attacks from heavily equipped gladiators, such as the Provocator gladiators. The fishing net was used to try to trip or entangle an opponent. The trident, a spear with three points, was usually used by fishermen.

Special fighters

◀ The equite gladiators began their combat on horseback, but if one fell off his horse, the other had to fight on foot as well.

446 Equite gladiators were equipped in the same way as the Roman army's cavalry. They used a small, leather shield, a medium-length sword and a lance about 2.5 metres long. Only the helmet was different from that of the army. The army helmet had an open face and no brim. Whenever these gladiators appeared in a show, they were the first to fight.

447 Female gladiators were rare. They first appeared around AD 55 in Rome as a novelty act. They fought only against other women or animals. Female gladiators were banned in AD 200.

▲ Female gladiators fought in the same style as the male gladiators.

448 **The andabatae (an-dab-AH-tie) fought blindfolded.** The Romans loved anything new or unusual. Andabatae gladiators wore helmets with no eye-holes. They listened carefully for sounds of their opponent, then attacked with two swords. Sometimes the andabatae would fight on horseback.

449 **British gladiators fought from chariots.** Known as the essedarii (ess-e-DAH-ree-ee), meaning chariot-man, these gladiators first appeared after Julius Caesar invaded Britain in 55 BC. The first chariot gladiators were prisoners of war.

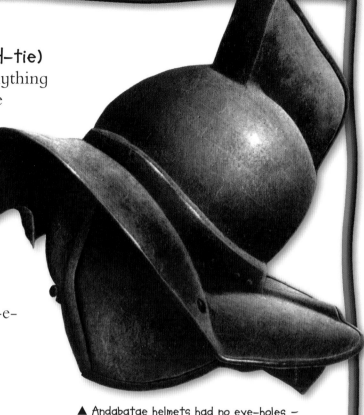

▲ Andabatae helmets had no eye-holes – the gladiators had to rely on their hearing.

ANDABATAE FIGHT

Recreate the combat of the andabatae with this game

You will need:

blindfold   four or more players

1. One player is the andabatae. Tie on the blindfold, making sure the player can see nothing.

2. Other players run around the andabatae calling out their name.

3. The andabatae tries to catch someone. When they catch a person, that person puts on the blindfold and becomes the andabatae. The game continues for as long as you like.

450 **Special clowns who fought with wooden weapons were known as paegniarii (payeg-nee-AH-ree-ee).** They appeared at shows during gaps between gladiator fights. They were skilled acrobats and would sometimes tell jokes or make fun of important people in the audience.

► The paegniarii used wooden weapons and put on comic displays to entertain the crowd between gladiator fights.

Recruiting gladiators

AUGUSTUS

JULIUS

SPARTACUS

CLAUDIUS

451 The first gladiators were household slaves. The will of the dead man who was being honoured by the games would name his slaves who were to fight. They were made to fight during the funeral. Those who were killed were then buried with their owner.

SPQR

CASSIUS SCRIBONIUS

CRIME
ROBBERY

SENTENCE
THREE YEARS
AS GLADIATOR

◄ When convicted, the name, crime and sentence of each criminal was inscribed on a tablet.

▲ Before a show, the names of the gladiators who were to fight were written on a scroll.

452 Criminals could be sent to the arena. The Romans did not have prisons so criminals were usually fined, flogged or executed. Men guilty of some crimes might be ordered to become gladiators for a set period of time – such as three years for robbery. These men would be given a tablet showing the details of their crime and sentence.

I DON'T BELIEVE IT!

When the lanista wanted to buy slaves to become gladiators, he would choose big, strong men. On average a gladiator was about 5 centimetres taller than an ordinary Roman.

453 **Some gladiators were volunteers.** These volunteers had often been former soldiers who wanted to earn money for their retirement. They signed up for a period of time or for a set number of fights and received a large payment of money if they survived.

454 **Gladiators were recruited by the lanista.** Every gladiator school was run by the lanista, the owner and chief trainer. The lanista decided who to recruit and how to train them. He would choose the strongest men to fight in heavy armour and the quickest men to fight as Retiarius gladiators.

◄ Slaves for sale were paraded in front of potential buyers. They were sold to the highest bidder.

455 **Strong slaves were sold to become gladiators.** In ancient Rome, slaves were treated as property, and had no human rights. If a man wanted to raise money, he might sell a slave. The lanista would pay a high price for strong male slaves. Many young slaves were also sold to become gladiators.

► The price of slaves varied, but a slave might cost about the same as an average workman's wages for a year.

Learning to fight

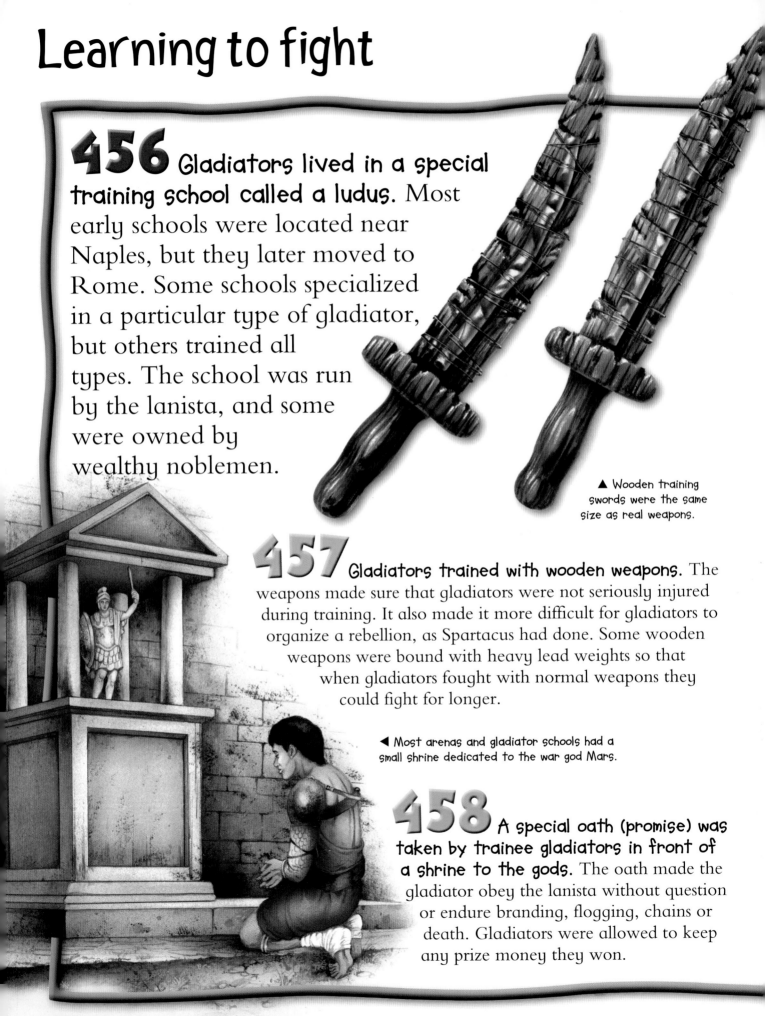

456 Gladiators lived in a special training school called a ludus. Most early schools were located near Naples, but they later moved to Rome. Some schools specialized in a particular type of gladiator, but others trained all types. The school was run by the lanista, and some were owned by wealthy noblemen.

▲ Wooden training swords were the same size as real weapons.

457 Gladiators trained with wooden weapons. The weapons made sure that gladiators were not seriously injured during training. It also made it more difficult for gladiators to organize a rebellion, as Spartacus had done. Some wooden weapons were bound with heavy lead weights so that when gladiators fought with normal weapons they could fight for longer.

◄ Most arenas and gladiator schools had a small shrine dedicated to the war god Mars.

458 A special oath (promise) was taken by trainee gladiators in front of a shrine to the gods. The oath made the gladiator obey the lanista without question or endure branding, flogging, chains or death. Gladiators were allowed to keep any prize money they won.

459 New trainees fought against a wooden post called a palus. A trainer, known as a doctor, taught the recruits how to use their weapons and shields to strike at the 2-metre-high wooden post. Only when the basic tactics had been learned did the recruits practise against other gladiators.

▼ Gladiators trained for several hours every day, being instructed on fighting techniques by retired gladiators and more experienced men.

460 The buildings of a gladiator school were constructed around a square training ground. This was where the gladiators did most of their training, exercises and other activities. Around the training ground were rooms where the gladiators lived. Recruits slept in dormitories, but fully trained gladiators had their own rooms.

Armour, shields and helmets

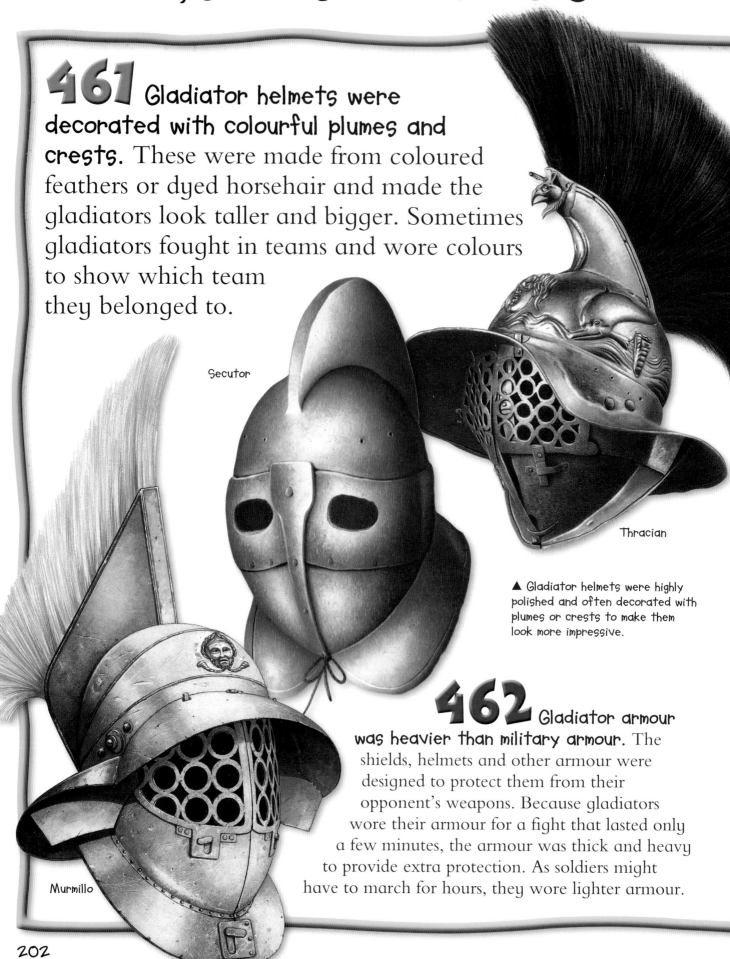

461 **Gladiator helmets were decorated with colourful plumes and crests.** These were made from coloured feathers or dyed horsehair and made the gladiators look taller and bigger. Sometimes gladiators fought in teams and wore colours to show which team they belonged to.

Secutor

Thracian

▲ Gladiator helmets were highly polished and often decorated with plumes or crests to make them look more impressive.

462 Gladiator armour was heavier than military armour. The shields, helmets and other armour were designed to protect them from their opponent's weapons. Because gladiators wore their armour for a fight that lasted only a few minutes, the armour was thick and heavy to provide extra protection. As soldiers might have to march for hours, they wore lighter armour.

Murmillo

463 Some armour was covered with gold.

Most gladiator armour was decorated with carvings and reliefs of gods such as Mars, god of war, or Victory, goddess of success. These decorations were often coated with thin sheets of pure gold.

464 Padded armour was worn on the arms and legs.

Thick layers of cloth and padding gave protection from glancing blows from the weapons or from being hit by the shield of the opponent.

Final shape

Leather binding

Cloth padding

▲ Gladiator shields were painted and decorated with gold to impress the audience.

▲ Arms and legs were often covered with layers of woollen cloth tied on with leather bindings.

465 The body was usually left without any armour at all.

This meant that a single blow could kill them, or injure them so seriously that they had to ask for mercy. Gladiators needed to be skilful with both weapons and shields to survive.

I DON'T BELIEVE IT!

Gladiator helmets were very heavy – they weighed about 7 kilograms, twice as much as an army helmet!

A day in the life

466 Gladiators were woken at dawn to begin training. They had several servants to look after them, usually boys or old men. A servant would wake the gladiator at sunrise to make sure he was ready to begin his training on time.

▲ A gladiator would be awoken at dawn by one of the slaves owned by the training school.

467 Training lasted for hours each day. Even the most experienced gladiator began his day practising weapon strokes at a wooden post. This allowed the fighter to warm up, ready for the more serious training later in the day. Gladiators had special plain armour and blunt weapons to use when training.

▼ A stout wooden post about 2 metres tall was used for the more basic training exercises.

GLADIATOR MEAL

Ask an adult to help you prepare this gladiator meal.

You will need:

60 g rolled porridge oats
400 ml water pinch of salt
50 g ham 5 dried figs
2 tbsp olive oil
1 tsp dried rosemary.

1. Chop the ham and figs. Fry in the olive oil and rosemary.

2. Place the oats, water and salt in a saucepan. Bring to the boil, then simmer for 5 minutes.

3. When the oats have thickened, scatter over the ham and figs.

◀ Gladiators were given simple, nutritious food such as porridge, carrots and sausages to keep them fit and healthy.

468 Barley porridge was the usual food of gladiators, but they also ate meats, fruits and vegetables. The Romans believed that barley was a highly nutritious food that helped to build up muscles. The owner of the gladiator school did not waste money on fancy foods, but provided plain and healthy meals.

▼ Gladiators were sometimes given treatment by masseurs, doctors and other specialists who looked after their health.

469 Gladiators received regular massages. Romans knew that massages would help to ease stiff joints or relax muscles. Massages could be very helpful to old injuries. The gladiator school would employ at least one man who was an expert masseur to keep the gladiators in top condition.

470 Older, retired gladiators trained the new recruits. Gladiators who survived long enough to win their freedom often found jobs at gladiator schools. They were expert fighters and knew many tricks and special moves. They trained the new recruits to be expert fighters. This would please the crowd, and give the gladiator a better chance of surviving.

Get ready for the games

471 **The first decision when staging gladitorial games (munus) was how much money to spend.** The man who hosted the event was known as the editor. A munus was an expensive event but most editors wanted to put on the most impressive show possible. They would spend as much money as they could spare.

472 The editor would choose different features for his show. A lanista would be hired to organize the show. Together, they would decide how many gladiators would fight and how many musicians and other performers were needed. The lanista would make sure the event was a success.

▲ Musicians and dancers were popular at gladiator shows. Shows often included a parade of entertainers before the gladiators.

473 A dead gladiator cost more than a wounded one. The editor would sign a contract with the lanista. This set down everything that would appear at the munus and the cost. If a gladiator was killed, a special payment was made so that the lanista could buy and train a replacement. Many editors granted mercy to a wounded man to avoid paying extra.

474

Everything was hired — even the clothes worn by the organizer. The editor would hire expensive clothes and jewellery for himself and his family. He wanted to make sure that they looked their best when they appeared at the games. The editor wanted to impress his fellow citizens and make sure they would vote for him.

▼ Smart clothes were hired for the editor and his family so that they could show off to the audience.

475

The star of the show was the editor. Everything was arranged so that the editor of the games looked as important as possible. As well as wearing special clothes, he was given the most prominent seat in the amphitheatre and all the gladiators and other performers bowed to him. He was paying for the show and wanted to make sure he got all the credit.

A laurel wreath signified an honour granted by the Roman government

A toga was a special item of clothing that indicated the wearer's rank within society

Gold jewellery indicated a family's wealth

Brightly coloured silk from China showed wealth and sophistication

Purple was the most expensive dye in ancient Rome

Showtime!

476 **Advertising for the show began days beforehand.** The lanista sent out slaves to paint signs on walls, while others shouted announcements on the street. The slaves told people when and where the show was and what it included. They also told them the name of the editor of the show.

477 **The show began with a parade, which was led into the arena by the editor.** He was dressed in beautiful clothes and often rode in a chariot. Behind him came the musicians playing lively tunes. Then came the gladiators, each followed by a slave who carried the gladiator's weapons and armour. Then came statues of gods including the war god Mars. Finally the servants, referees and other officials entered the arena.

478 **Gladiators were carefully paired against each other.** Before the show began, the editor and lanista would decide which gladiators would fight each other. The show would start with beginners fighting each other, with the expert veterans appearing towards the end of the show. The results would be shouted out by a herald and written on a sign, or tabella, at one end of the arena.

479 The probatio was a crucial ceremony. Before the first fight of the show, the editor and lanista would enter the arena for the probatio. This ceremony involved the men testing the weapons and armour to be used in the show. Swords were tested by slicing up vegetables, and armour by being hit with clubs.

◀ Each gladiator show began with a grand parade of everyone involved in the show, led by the editor in a chariot.

480 Musicians performed first. The band included trumpets, curved horns and the hydraulis. This was a loud instrument like a modern church organ. The musicians entertained the crowd between fights and played music during the show ceremonies.

TRUE OR FALSE?

1. The hydraulis was an instrument like a modern trumpet.
2. Weapons were tested before the show to make sure they were sharp.
3. Gladiators wore their armour during the opening parade.

Answers:
1. FALSE The hydraulis was an instrument like a modern organ 2. TRUE Weapons were tested during the probatio ceremony 3. FALSE Slaves carried the armour behind the gladiators

Water fights

481 Some gladiatorial shows took place on water. The most impressive of all were the naumachiae, or sea fights. For these shows, an artificial lake 557 metres long by 536 metres wide was dug beside the river Tiber. Small warships were brought up the river and launched on the lake when a sea fight was due to take place.

482 Naval fights were recreations of real battles. In 2 BC, Emperor Augustus staged a naumachia that recreated a battle fought 400 years earlier between the Greeks and the Persians. Emperor Titus staged a battle that originally started between the Greeks and Egyptians. These battles did not always end with the same winner as the real battle.

▼ Recreated naval battles were extremely expensive to stage, so didn't take place very often.

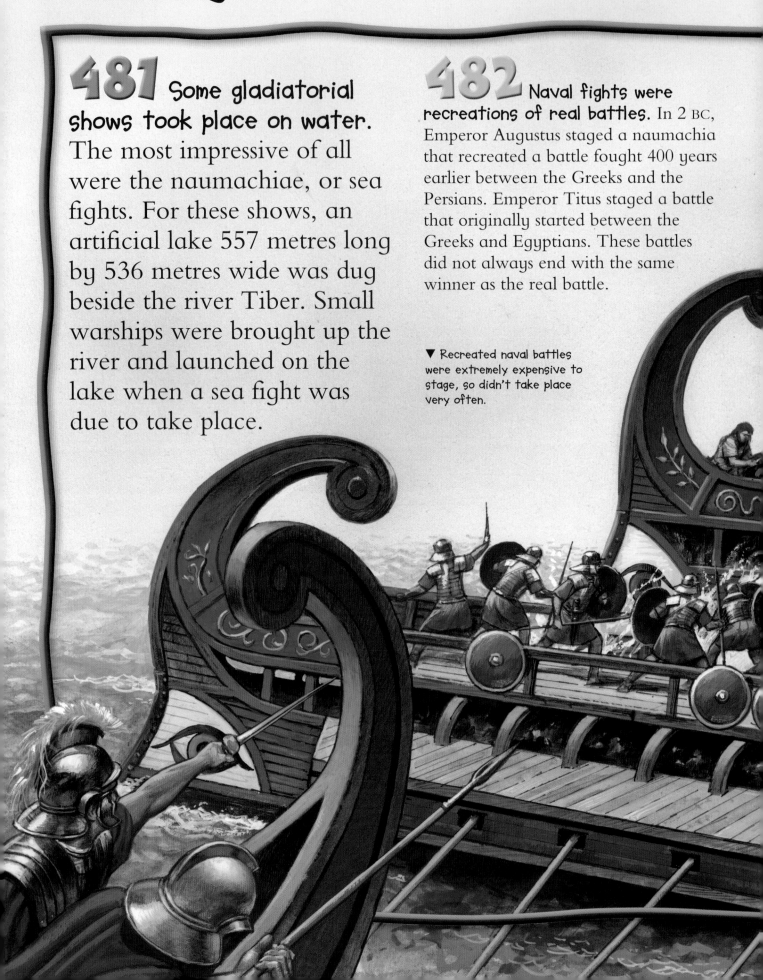

483

The first naval gladiators did not try to kill each other. The first of the sea battles were staged by Julius Caesar to celebrate a naval victory. The show was designed to impress the audience with the skills of the sailors and the way Caesar had won his victory.

484

One naval show involved 19,000 men. Emperor Claudius staged a sea battle on Lake Fucino. The men fighting were not sailors or gladiators but criminals condemned to death. Most of the men died and any survivors were sent to work as slaves.

485

The Colosseum in Rome could be flooded for naval fights. When the Colosseum was first built it had special pipes that could fill the arena with water and then drain it away again. The flooded arena was used for fights between special miniature warships crewed by gladiators. Later, the pipes were replaced by trapdoors and stage scenery.

I DON'T BELIEVE IT!

On one occasion, gladiators took one look at the poor condition of the warships and refused to board them.

Wild animal hunts

486 **The first wild animal show was to celebrate a military victory.** In 164 BC Rome defeated the powerful North African city of Carthage. The victorious general, Publius Cornelius Scipio, was given the nickname Africanus. He brought back to Rome hundreds of African wild animals, such as elephants, crocodiles and lions. After parading the animals through the streets, he included them in his gladiatorial games.

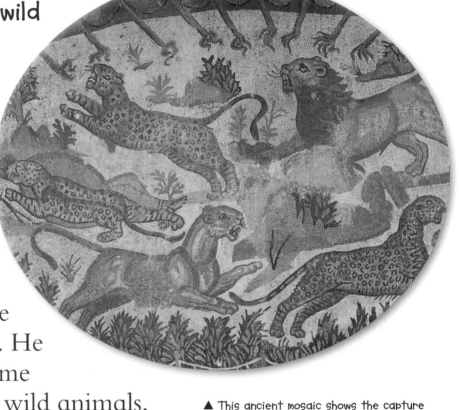

▲ This ancient mosaic shows the capture of wild animals, such as lions and gazelles. They were then shipped to Rome to fight in the arenas.

487 **One elephant hunt went badly wrong.** In 79 BC General Gnaeus Pompey staged a wild elephant hunt with 20 elephants in a temporary arena in Rome. The crowd was protected by a tall iron fence, but two of the elephants charged at the fence, smashing it down. The elephants were quickly killed by hunters, but several people were injured.

488 **The design of the arena changed to make it safer for the crowds.** As the wild animal shows became more popular, the need to keep the watching crowd safe meant changes to the arena had to be made. The arena was sunk about 3 metres into the ground and surrounded by a vertical wall of smooth stone. No animal could leap up the wall or break it down, so the spectators were safe from attack.

489 **Some animal shows were fantastic and strange.** The Romans loved to see animals fighting each other. Sometimes a group of lions or wolves would be set to attack zebras or deer. At other times two hunting animals would be made to fight each other. They were often chained together to encourage them to fight. Some pairings were very odd – a snake was set against a lion, a seal set to fight a wolf or a bull against a bear.

490 **One of the most popular animal fights was when a lion was set against a tiger.** So many lions and tigers were sent to Rome to die in the fights that they became extinct in some areas of North Africa and the Middle East.

I DON'T BELIEVE IT!

The Romans loved watching animals that had been trained to perform tricks. One animal trainer put on shows in which an ape drove a chariot pulled by camels.

▼ A wild tiger attacks a gladiator, as seen in the 2000 movie *Gladiator*. Wild animals were part of most arena shows.

Outside Rome

491 **More gladiators fought in southern Italy than in Rome.** The idea of gladiatorial fights came from Campania, the area of Italy around Naples. For hundreds of years, the gladiator schools in Campania produced the best-trained gladiators and had more than anywhere else. One school had over 5000 gladiators training at one time.

492 **The city of London had a small arena for gladiatorial games and other events.** It stood inside the city walls beside the army fortress, near what is now St Paul's Cathedral. The 30-metre-long amphitheatre was built of stone and timber and could seat around 4000 spectators. St Albans, Chester and Caerleon also had amphitheatres.

▼ The arena at Pompeii. The oval shape, banked seating and two exits were the common design for all arenas.

493 **All gladiatorial shows had to honour the emperor.** By about AD50, political power was in the hands of the emperor. It was the emperor who decided who could stand for election, and who would win the election. The editor of a gladiator show always began by dedicating the show to the emperor.

494 **The best gladiators were sent to Rome.** Gladiators who fought in provinces such as Britain or Spain were owned by lanistas who travelled from city to city to put on a show. Agents from Rome would watch these shows and any gladiator who was particularly good would be taken to Rome to fight in the the Colosseum.

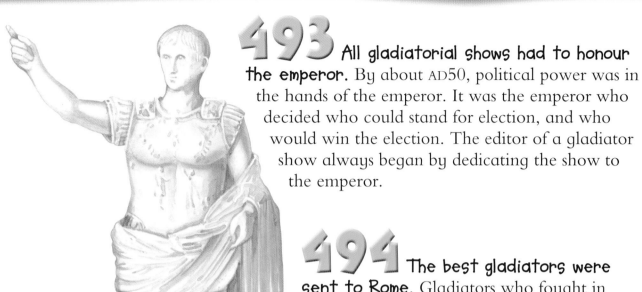

▶ A statue of an emperor. Such a statue stood in most arenas and other public buildings.

▼ A gladiator fight reaches its end, as seen in the 1960 movie *Spartacus*.

495 **Some towns banned gladiators.** Not everyone enjoyed the fights. Many Romans refused to attend the games. Some cities, particularly in Greece and the eastern provinces, did not have an amphitheatre and refused to put on combats. Some people thought the fights were a waste of good slaves.

The last gladiators

▲ A scene from the 2000 movie *Gladiator*. The bloodshed in gladiator fights appalled some Romans.

496 **Gladiatorial games became less and less popular.** Seneca, a wise man and a great thinker, wrote that attending the games made Romans more cruel and inhuman than they had been before. The writer Artemidorus of Daldis said that the games were dishonourable, cruel and wicked. However most Romans approved of the games and enjoyed watching them.

497 **In AD 324, Christian bishops tried to ban gladiatorial fights.** After AD 250, Christianity became popular in the Roman Empire. Christians believed that the fights were sinful and they asked Emperor Constantine I to ban the fights. He banned private games, but allowed state games to continue.

QUIZ

1. Which philosopher thought watching gladiator fights made people cruel?
2. Which emperor closed down the gladiator schools in Rome?
3. Which emperor banned private gladiatorial games?

Answers:
1. Seneca 2. Emperor Honorius
3. Emperor Constantine I

498 In AD 366 Pope Damasus used gladiators to murder rival churchmen. When Pope Liberius died the cardinals of Rome could not agree on a successor. Followers who wanted Ursinus to be the next pope were meeting in the church of St Maria Trastevere when Damasus hired a gang of gladiators to attack them. The gladiators broke into the church and killed 137 people. Damasus then became pope.

▲ Heavily armed gladiators were sometimes hired by ambitious politicians and churchmen to murder their rivals.

499 The Christian monk Telemachus was the first to stop a gladiator fight. During a show in the Colosseum in AD 404, Telemachus forced apart two fighting gladiators. He made a speech asking for the shows to stop, but angry spectators killed him. Emperor Honorius then closed down all the gladiator schools in Rome.

500 The last gladiators fought in around AD 445. In AD 410, the city of Rome was captured by a tribe of barbarians. The Roman Empire was falling to pieces. People were too busy trying to escape invasions or to earn a living to organize gladiatorial fights.

◄ The monk Telemachus managed to stop a gladiator fight, but paid for his actions with his life.

INDEX

ACKNOWLEDGEMENTS

The publishers would like to thank the following sources for the use of their photographs:

t = top, b = bottom, l = left, r = right, c = centre, bg = background, m = main

Cover: *Front* (t) Laurence Gough/Shutterstock.com, (b) Robert Harding Productions/Glow Images, MAEADV/ Shutterstock.com; *Spine* Laurence Gough/Shutterstock.com; *Back* (t) Olga Meffista/Shutterstock.com, (b) MitarArt/ Shutterstock.com

Alamy 30 Miguel Cuenca; 103 Charles Stirling (Diving); 133(br) Aliki Sapountzi/Aliki Image Library; 136(b) Caro; 142(cr) The Art Archive

Corbis 25 PoodlesRock; 56 Christophe Boisvieux; 84(b) Remigiusz Sikora/epa; 113(t) The Art Archive; 125 Richard Cummins; 126–127 Jose Fuste Raga; 134–135 Vanni Archive; 148(bl) Roger Wood; 149(tr) Mimmo Jodice; 158(bl) Alfredo Dagli Orti/The Art Archive; 159 Farrell Grehan; 170 Araldo de Luca; 171 Richard Baker/In Pictures; 174 Arne Hodalic; 175 Roger Ressmeyer; 176 Bettmann; 184 Bettmann; 212 Roger Wood; 214 K M Westermann

Dover 148–149(tc)

Fotolia.com 11 Konstantin Sutyagin

Glow Images 42(b) SuperStock; 47(b) Werner Forman Archive

National Geographic Creative 32–33(b) H.M. Herget; 38–39 H.M. Herget; 43 H.M. Herget; 46–47 H.M. Herget;

Photolibrary 57(t)

Pictorial Press 213 Dreamworks/Universal; 215 Bryna/Universal; 216 Dreamworks/Universal

Rex Features 113(bl) Patrick Frilet; 127 KPA/Zuma

Science Photo Library 20–21 Henning Dalhoff

Shutterstock.com 11 ChameleonsEye; 12(bg) diversepixel; 12–13(b) leoks; 16–17(bg) diversepixel; 18–19(bg) mountainpix; 36–37(bg) Luisa Fumi; 44(b) Architecteur; 45(b) Vladimir Korostyshevskiy; 44–45(bg) Eugene Sergeev; 48–49 WitR; 134(heading panel rt) Anelina, (fact panel rt) PaulPaladin; 134–135(label panels) Pakhnyushcha; 135(caption panel) David M. Schrader; 136(heading panel rt) Konstanttin; 136–137(bg) Vitaly Korovin; 137(fact panel) Apostrophe, (b) Filip Fuxa; 138(heading panel) haveseen, (caption panel rt); 138–139(bg) Luba V Nel, Valentin Agapov; 141(t) Ariy, (fact panel cl) Jaywarren79, (b&bg rt) Ev Thomas; 142(heading panel rt) aopsan; 142–143(panel bgs) Vitaly Korovin, (tc) Yulia Davidovich, (tr) Dionisvera; 143(herbs & spices, clockwise from tl) Noraluca013, Imageman, Robyn Mackenzie, Madlen, Volosina, (vegetables, clockwise from tl) Vladyslav Danilin, Valentyn Volkov, Dulce Rubia, Jiang Hongyan, Madlen, eye-blink, (cr) picturepartners; 144–145(bg) Tischenko Irina, (br) James Steidl, (b) Bill McKelvie; 145(c,rt) Lora liu; 146(heading panel) Valentin Agapov; 146–147(bg rt) Andre Viegas; 151 (flowers, herbs & spices, clockwise from tl) M.Khebra, Aleksandra Duda, Africa Studio, Eric Gevaert; 152–153(bg) mg1408; 152(t); 153(tr) Viacheslav Lopatin; 156(heading panel rt) Vitaly Korovin; 157(t panel) ImageState, (tr) Iakov Kalinin; 158(l panel) donatas1205; 159(br, top to bottom) Paul Picone, Chris Hill, I. Pilon, (tr panel) Molodec; 160–161(bg) Javier Rosano; 162 Piotr Zajc; 164–165(bg) javarman; 166–167(bg) RoyStudio.eu; 170–171(bg) donatas1205; 170(panel t) bomg, (panel c) Clipart deSIGN; 172 JeniFoto, 174–175 khd; 175(r) jps

Superstock 139 imagebroker.net; 143 DeAgostini; 150(tr) Universal Images Group; 155(br) Album/Prisma/Album; 158–159(t) Universal Images Group; 163 DeAgostini; 164 DeAgostini; 165 J.D. Dallet/age fotostock; 167 Image Asset Management Ltd.; 169 Robert Harding Picture Library

Topfoto 25(t) The Granger Collection; 28(t) The Granger Collection; 45(t) 2005; 58 Topham Picturepoint; 60(t/r) The British Museum/HIP; 72 TopFoto; 73(t) Topham Picturepoint; 76(t) Topham Picturepoint; 80(b) Werner Forman Archive/The Greenland Museum; 82(t) Topham Picturepoint; 82(b) Charles Walker; 83(c) Fortean/Trottmann; 85(t) Charles Walker, (b) Roger-Viollet; 86(b); 87(b) TopFoto/Fotean; 88 Topham Picturepoint; 89(c) TopFoto/HIP; 90(c) RIA Novosti; 91(b) Topham Picturepoint; 100 Topham Picturepoint; 108–109 TopFoto; 146–147(tc) AAAC; 147(cr) The Granger Collection; 155(bl) The Granger Collection; 159(bl) The Granger Collection

All other photographs are from: digitalSTOCK, digitalvision, Dreamstime.com, ImageState, iStockphoto.com, John Foxx, PhotoAlto, PhotoDisc, PhotoEssentials, PhotoPro, Stockbyte

All artworks from the Miles Kelly Artwork Bank

Every effort has been made to acknowledge the source and copyright holder of each picture. Miles Kelly Publishing apologises for any unintentional errors or omissions.